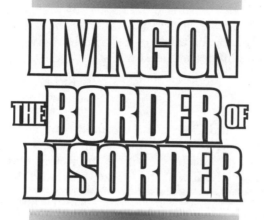

LIVING ON THE BORDER OF DISORDER

"The loss of Karen Carpenter was a terrible tragedy for us all. The music industry and her fans around the world will never be the same. Her struggle with eating disorders was long and difficult, and in her final months she reached out to Cherry Boone O'Neill for help and hope. Cherry and her husband, Dan, lived through and conquered this devastating illness faced by so many today. Their book, *Living on the Border of Disorder*, is a powerful and timely tool for those of us who have lived on that border. I highly recommend it."

Richard Carpenter
songwriter/musician

"I know Dan and Cherry, and the life-threatening struggle they have survived. What they learned offers a practical and healthy approach . . . both to the victims of disorder and to those who live in the 'network' around them."

Cathy Rigby McCoy
Olympic gymnast

"Cherry's disorder was heartwrenching, devastating to our whole family. We tried so hard to help—by loving, caring, and praying. And yet we often felt so painfully powerless. As Cherry and Dan discovered a pathway of healing, the simple but effective steps they learned brought new health to Cherry, and stronger relationships between us all."

Pat Boone

How to Cope With an Addictive Person

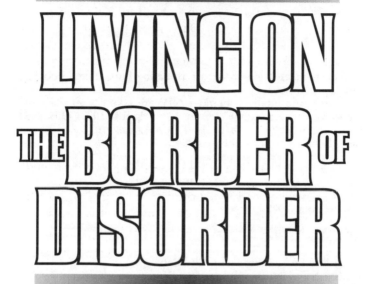

LIVING ON THE BORDER OF DISORDER

Cherry Boone O'Neill
AND Dan O'Neill
WITH PAUL THIGPEN

BETHANY HOUSE PUBLISHERS
MINNEAPOLIS, MINNESOTA 55438

Published by Bethany House Publishers
A Ministry of Bethany Fellowship, Inc.
6820 Auto Club Road, Minneapolis, Minnesota 55438

Printed in the United States of America

Library of Congress Cataloging-in-Publication Data
O'Neill, Cherry Boone, 1954-
   Living on the border of disorder / Cherry Boone O'Neill and Dan O'Neill
      p. cm.
   Includes bibliographical references.

   1. Compulsive behavior—Patients—Family relationships.
2. Compulsive behavior—Treatment—Social aspects.
3. Codependency.
4. Compulsive behavior—Religious aspects—Christianity.
I. O'Neill, Dan, 1948-   . II. Title.
   RC533.054 1992
   616.86—dc20   92-10183
   ISBN 1–55661–262–1   CIP

This book is dedicated to
the "border people" in our lives
who have shared healing with us
through their love, honesty and compassion:

Pat and Shirley Boone
Bill and Melba O'Neill
Dan and Chrissie Ganfield
Ray and Joanne Vath

DAN O'NEILL AND CHERRY BOONE O'NEILL have multifaceted careers that include over fifteen published books. Dan is the president of Messenger Communications and co-founder of Mercy Corps International. The daughter of Pat and Shirley Boone, Cherry is an experienced entertainer and songwriter whose recovery from anorexia nervosa became a national story. They make a home for their son and three daughters in Redmond, Washington.

The following friends have greatly contributed to this manuscript:

Paul Thigpen, co-writer
David Hazard, editor
Ray Vath, M.D. consulting medical editor

Preface

Early in my medical training, I observed that patients would often come into the hospital very ill, but after a few days or weeks would recover quite rapidly. All too often, however, they would return in a short time, again in need of treatment. I wondered what was happening after they left the hospital and soon discovered that others were asking the same question.

Then I came across the writings of Virginia Satir in *Conjoint Family Therapy*. Fortunately, I was able to observe her in action. Through this experience I learned that to keep a patient well, I needed to teach the family how to become part of the treatment team. I learned how deeply important it is for the patient to be discharged into a healing environment. After that, relapses into unhealthy behavior diminished significantly.

Alcoholics Anonymous had already discovered this therapeutic need, establishing Alanon for the non-drinking spouse, and milieu therapy was appearing in the psychiatric literature. One problem with the psychiatric approach was that it was based on a subtle search for blame. Schizophrenia, for example, was blamed on the double-binding, schizophrenogenic mother. Obsessive-compulsive disorder was thought to be due to severe, rigid toilet training. This is why so many parents ask me, "Doctor, what did we do wrong?" bracing themselves for harsh criticism. Wouldn't a better question be: "What did you do, and what happened when you did it?" That would lead to a search for cause, and encourage an attitude more positively directed toward searching for a better way to relate.

The non-judgmental approach of Alanon can be seen in the biblical injunction: "Do not judge others lest you be judged" (Matthew 7:1, NASB). Christ accurately identified the problem when on the cross He said, "Father, forgive them for they know not what they do!" This indicates that the real enemy is ignorance of health-giving lifestyles, and that therapy is best when it is educational. Even Sigmund Freud said therapy is a re-educative process. When this approach is used, even the most severe of mental illness responds, as demonstrated by McFarlane and Dunne in their work with families with a schizophrenic member.

In the psychoeducational approach, the first step in family therapy is to observe the interactional pattern: What does the power structure look like? Who is speaking to whom? What deeper message is conveyed by both disagreements and silences? What is the style of language? Then attention is drawn to the responses to words and actions. If responses are negative, then healthier alternatives are suggested, explored, and evaluated.

As the reader shares the real-life experiences of Dan and Cherry O'Neill in identifying the patterns that were not working for them, you may come to understand the messages that have been conveyed to you by people in your own life. As the maladaptive patterns are identified, hopefully you will feel relief rather than guilt. Any dread you may feel can then be replaced with curiosity and a sense of adventure as you discover new ways to interact.

In my own book on eating disorders, *Counseling Those with Eating Disorders*, I identify several factors that I believe are present in the life of an eating-disordered patient. Those with which the family can be most helpful include identity clarification and the replacement of the power struggle with collaboration.

The cure for perfectionism is unconditional love; for low self-esteem, forgiveness. In our work we have used Harry S. Sullivan's definition of love: *a condition that exists when another person's well-being and security are as important as your own.* Forgiveness is defined as *the renunciation of resentment and the desire to punish.* Indeed, if these two learnable skills alone were taught to families, many of the problems affecting individuals, families, and communities would be radically reduced. Dan and Cherry learned through their struggle that they could love each other unconditionally, and as a necessary part of that process they learned to forgive each other unconditionally.

Often I hear a patient's family member state emphatically, "I'm not going to change!" But behind that statement is usually a simple lack of awareness of what the alternatives are. When the Bible promises us that "those who hunger and thirst after righteousness will be satisfied," it states a great principle of personal growth. Dan and Cherry possessed this thirst even before they met me, and this strong desire, coupled with quick minds to grasp these concepts, facilitated Cherry's surprisingly rapid recovery from her eating disorder. Dan and Cherry's families also searched for better ways of relating with Cherry, and this certainly aided the process. Their experience illustrates that when people of good will work together to find better solutions to life's problems, the solutions will be found. The good news is that this is only the beginning of a process of growth that has continued to the present and has become a way of life for the future as well. The result has been health not only for the O'Neills, but physical, emotional, familial, social, occupational, and spiritual health for the many other lives they touch.

Although the work that Dan and Cherry have accomplished may at times sound simple, it is important to remember that change is always stressful, with the stress proportional to the degree of change and the rate of change. The O'Neills succeeded because both were willing to face their fears of the unknown, such as leaving successful jobs in California to face treatment in Washington, and living through the depression that results from grieving the loss of old familiar ways, even those that lead to suffering. Furthermore, when the inexperience of attempting new strategies occasionally failed, discouragement did, at times, set in. The power of having a social network involved in change is that when we are tempted to become discouraged, others will support us in our times of trouble and give us hope that we will attain the prize if we don't grow weary.

As you embark upon the journey this book offers, it is my sincere hope that Dan and Cherry's story will create a hunger for growth in your life; and if you are a person living on the border of disorder, the resulting change will cause others in your life to grow as well. For if you remove the beam from your own eye, you will see more clearly to help others.

Raymond E. Vath, M.D.

Contents

Life on the Border

—Dan

The wedding was only a few weeks away. Cherry Boone and I were deeply in love, thrilled at the prospect of a new life together. For each of us, the past held mistakes and the present had its own set of problems; but we'd confessed those to each other, and we knew we could build a happy future.

Cherry's confession had included the revelation that she struggled with eating disorders. For years she had battled anorexia nervosa, a condition characterized by an obsession with weight loss and self-starvation. By the time of our engagement, her anorexia had given way to yet another condition called bulimia: the ugly habit of binge eating, followed by purges of self-induced vomiting and laxative abuse.

I knew that Cherry's parents, Pat and Shirley Boone, were aware of her struggles and were trying to help her. They had sought the assistance of doctors, nutritionists, pastors, and even people with healing ministries. But they had only been able to find out very little about the true nature and complexity of the problem. They found it mysterious and perplexing.

In fact, few other people at the time knew much about eating disorders. Anorexia and bulimia were hardly ever discussed in public back then—it was 1975—though both disorders are surprisingly common in America and are potentially fatal. Not having read much about eating disorders myself, I didn't quite understand how a seemingly well-balanced woman like Cherry, who had expressed a strong Christian spirituality, could have such a bizarre and destructive problem.

Nevertheless, at the time I wasn't too worried because her weight was close to normal. We had discussed her struggles, and I had helped her with some suggestions about how to eat "normally." Our blossoming friendship was refreshingly open and honest, so I was confident that we could overcome any problem we might face. With my encouragement and support, she seemed to be achieving control of the behavior.

At least, that's what I thought.

One night I brought Cherry home after sharing an enjoyable dinner at a fine restaurant. As we stood outside the back door—the one that led into her family's laundry room next to their kitchen—I reminded her that after such a full meal, she had no need to eat anything else before she went to bed. I was concerned that, alone in the kitchen late at night, she would be tempted to binge.

"Now just go right through that kitchen and upstairs to your room," I insisted. "Promise me you'll go straight to bed. No more food."

She promised, and I had every reason to believe she would keep her word. So after we kissed, I turned to leave as she shut the door.

But then I hesitated. I knew she seemed to depend on me often those days to help her set some boundaries on her food consumption. *Maybe*, I thought, *I'd better check just to make sure she's gone up to her room without succumbing to the many temptations stashed in the kitchen.*

I stepped back up to the door and peered through its small window. Cherry was still there, squatting near the door.

And eating out of the dog dish.

There she was, gnawing on a leftover lamb chop that had been left for the dog, stuffing the meat in her mouth as fast as she could rip it from the bone. I was flooded with anger, disgust, and disbelief—and I pounded on the window.

Cherry looked up and, in horror, saw me watching her. She opened the door, trembling. Caught in the act! I pounded her with questions.

"What do you think you're doing?" I shouted. *"Doesn't your word mean anything?"*

Cherry dissolved into tears and, trembling, sobbed out apologies. But to me, they sounded hollow. *It's bad enough that she was eating dog scraps,* I thought. *But she just made a promise to me and then broke it within seconds. This is the woman I'm planning to marry?* I thought to myself. *Better think again. This is a most troubling turn of events.*

I turned and walked away into the darkness, not knowing whether I would return.

—Cherry

When Dan left my house that night, I was devastated. Never before and never since have I felt the depths of depression and despair I experienced during the following few days. After watching Dan walk away from me—possibly forever, for all I knew—I collapsed into a heap, moaning and in tears.

I felt shock and shame. I knew I had promised Dan I would resist the urge to eat, but like so many times before, I simply couldn't seem to stop it. I wanted to be free of my binging and purging; I hated myself whenever I gave in and did it. So why couldn't I control myself?

The full weight of my actions suddenly came crashing down on me. I felt alienated from Dan and disillusioned with myself. I grieved for what seemed to be the death of our relationship, the death of my honor, of my self-respect—the death of hope. Everything looked bleak, and I felt trapped in a nightmare, an inner "twilight zone" where nothing made sense.

—Dan

As it turned out, I did return to Cherry's home the next day. Not knowing what else to do, I gave her a stern lecture.

We also went on with the wedding as planned, but our relationship was seriously marred. I had taken the incident as a personal betrayal. It was years before I would learn to trust her fully again.

Today, after finding our way along the path of recovery, we are able to smile at the "dog dish episode." We've told the story many times on nationally televised interviews, in Cherry's best-selling book *Starving for Attention*,[1] and to the thousands of people who have called or written us for help in dealing with compulsive disorders. We can laugh because Cherry was able to overcome her destructive behaviors with the help of a loving, caring network of people who surrounded us.

Nevertheless, we went down a few blind alleys on the way to healing. Many of them stemmed from my confidence that I could help Cherry find a simple, direct way to overcome her disorder. I tried a number of approaches, and some of them even seemed to work temporarily. But in the end, none of them provided her with lasting success.

First, I listened patiently and supportively when she initially confessed her problem to me. I prayed with her and reassured her that she would find victory in her struggle. I encouraged Cherry to stop striving to accomplish so much, to concentrate on "being" instead of on "doing." This approach was all good in itself, but it only helped her briefly.

Second, I stressed the importance of our shared faith. I listed spiritual insights I thought would make a positive difference in her life—a kind of formula for success.

Third, I drew up a regimented eating plan for Cherry that deliberately excluded any food that triggered her binges. For a while she convinced me she was following it, but when the evidence began to accumulate that she wasn't, I checked up on her and confronted her, urging her to stay in control.

Fourth, when Cherry's weight plunged to eighty pounds, I put her in the hospital. The physical ravages of her bulimic behavior had become a serious threat to her health. Radical measures seemed warranted. Within ten days she gained a few pounds back; but only the symptoms of her problem had been addressed. The real root

---

[1]Cherry Boone O'Neill, *Starving for Attention*, Updated and re-released (Minneapolis, Minn.: CompCare Publishers, LifeCare imprint, 1992).

causes remained untouched by surface strategies.

Of course, I meant well. I wanted Cherry to be healthy, happy, and free of her problem. But I was mistaken in thinking that it was somehow within my power to "fix" things for her. It was only when we found a psychotherapist who exposed the roots of her compulsion that she was able to make genuine, lasting progress toward recovery.

The road to wholeness was tough, and it was just as difficult for the people around Cherry as it was for Cherry herself. When I recall the dog dish story, I remember all too well how confused and angry I felt that night. In the following months, I discovered that living on the border of someone else's disorder can be frightening and frustrating. Mistrust, misunderstanding, resentment, and fear all take their toll on us when someone we love seems committed to a path of self-destruction.

Living Near the "Epicenter"

Millions of people are struggling in their own private hell, trapped in circumstances very similar to ours. This book is for them. You're a "border" person if someone you care for deeply is caught in any of a number of bondages:

alcoholism
drug abuse
bulimia
anorexia
overeating
sexual addiction
manic depression
pornography
compulsive gambling
compulsive stealing or lying
other obsessive-compulsive behaviors

These destructive habits can be summed up under the term *impulse control disorders*—the tendency to gratify one's immediate desires or express one's immediate impulse to act, without regard to consequences.[2] When an impulse control disorder becomes entrenched, its health-threatening behavior patterns have ripple effects far beyond the disordered person's own life, hurting associates, friends, and relatives and drawing them into a painful emotional web.

Compare an impulse control disorder to an earthquake. Its occurrence, timing, and magnitude cannot be predicted. The disordered person is the "epicenter"—using our seismic analogy—where the worst damage is done and the destruction is most immediately apparent. But radiating out from the epicenter are concentric circles of damage as well: the people whose lives are relationally adjacent to the disordered person. The closer they stand to the center, the more devastated they will be.

What does it feel like to be a "border" person? Here are some emotions you may struggle with yourself:

Distress. Typically, when you must cope with a disordered friend or family member you initially feel a deep concern over the situation. The more you love the person, the greater your pain knowing that she has lost control of life and is careening down a self-destructive, potentially fatal road. You may also be saddened and disturbed by the destructive effects you see in the lives of other "border" people—many of whom may also be close to you—who must also cope with your loved one.

Anger. Perhaps more than anything else you feel angry. Your hostility may range from mild frustration to violent rage. The night I saw Cherry eating from the dog dish, I was so furious I could hardly speak. From my perspective, she had broken an important promise—one she could easily have kept. I felt offended, insulted, betrayed.

Multiply that episode by a thousand and you create an emotional climate of bitterness. To you it's clear that the habit is destructive, and you're convinced that all the offender has to do is exert some willpower to quit. The failure to stop, therefore, seems inexcusable, perverse, stubborn. The anger mounts as you ask yourself, "Why is he

---

[2]Robert M. Goldenson, Ph.D., ed., *Longman Dictionary of Psychology and Psychiatry* (New York: Longman, 1984), p. 370.

doing this to me? Why can't she just control herself? Can't he see he's killing himself, and wounding us as well?"

Nor is the anger directed only at the disordered person. You may feel angry with a counselor or doctor who fails to help. You may berate yourself for being helpless to fix the problem. And you may experience a vague, unfocused anger at the prevailing circumstances in general.

Doubt. You may arrive at an interior crisis of faith— faith in yourself, in others, in God. When goodwill, good ideas, and deeply held spirituality fail to achieve positive results, doubt may envelop you like a dark cloud, precipitating its own secondary anxiety.

Guilt. You feel guilty because you are powerless to control the other person's behavior, or because you sense that somehow you have actually contributed to the problem.

Fear. You fear for the disordered person's health. You fear losing him altogether. You also fear for the health and safety of others involved—including yourself. What if she gets high on drugs and beats the kids? What if he drives drunk and kills someone on the highway? What if she contracts AIDS and passes it on to you?

And you fear exposure. If you depend on the problem person for income, you fear the exposure could cause economic disaster. If you're responsible for the medical bills, they may overwhelm you financially. You may even fear for your own psychological health as you struggle to comprehend the staggering and painful events unfolding around you. The potential consequences for everyone involved are terrifying.

Confusion. You second-guess yourself repeatedly: Should I be confronting and threatening the person or just hope and pray things will get better? Should I take control of the situation or take a hands-off approach? Where do I go for help? What exactly is my responsibility, and what will work? If you have tried several responses and all have failed, the confusion intensifies.

Emotional exhaustion. As you wrestle—for months, or even years with confusion, doubt, fear, and anger, you grow weary. You feel perpetually tired and distracted. Your job performance suffers as your thoughts repeatedly return to the disordered person.

Is she having another martini with lunch? Is he betting this week's paycheck at the office pool? Anxious thoughts seem to multiply within you.

Mistrust. Perhaps the most damaging effect of a disorder on border people is the way it undermines your trust in the disordered person. She has lied to you repeatedly to cover up her habit; every shred of credibility is gone. So you feel compelled to spy, to snare her in a lie, to challenge the truthfulness of any statement she makes.

When Cherry's bulimia was at its worst, she would plan her binges carefully around the time I would be at work. As soon as I'd leave the house, she would lock the door, close the blinds, and make herself a calorie-packed chocolate drink in the blender. She would subsequently vomit the concoction. One morning I returned home unexpectedly to get something I'd forgotten, and I interrupted her in the middle of her secret binge. Understandably, I began to wonder every day what she might be doing behind my back.

Not surprisingly, under the crushing weight of all these negative feelings, the disordered person's relationships with those nearby are often fractured—or irretrievably broken. Marriages dissolve, families fragment, friends are lost, even professional helpers may become alienated. And the disorder itself only grows worse as the people who can contribute the most to healing grow disillusioned and distant.

The Best Chance for Recovery

I haven't painted such a desperate picture of life on the border to discourage you, or to repeat what you already know all too well. Instead, I hope you find it somewhat comforting to realize that you're not alone. People who must cope with disordered loved ones are often unaware just how common their circumstances are. Obsessive-compulsive behaviors may seem so bizarre that if you've never encountered them before, you may mistakenly assume your situation is unique. And if you haven't yet disclosed the problem to anyone else, you may feel isolated and imprisoned by it.

More importantly, I want to assure you there is hope—no matter how hopeless the situation seems right now. Our experience suggests that those living with disordered people are not doomed to waging a lifelong war of damage control. Though you may feel trapped by the problem, and may in fact have actually contributed to that problem, we believe you can regain control and balance while providing the disordered person with a positive environment for healthy change.

In fact, a great deal of evidence from the work of psychotherapists points to a single critical reality: *Disordered people have the best chance for recovery when they are surrounded by a loving, nurturing, supportive network of healthy relationships.* Medication, which helped Cherry and is often necessary to assist in recovery, cannot by itself assure long-term success. Insights into the nature of the disorder and its genesis are essential in forging the tools of recovery. But even they alone are not usually sufficient in securing total recovery. The power to use those tools for change—in fact, the very desire to change itself—is generated by the dynamo of healthy human relationships characterized by empathy, honesty, and love.

No doubt the "tremor zone" around a disorder seems an unlikely place to cultivate wholesome patterns of interaction. Our natural and learned impulses are to react to the disordered person with judgment, accusation, rejection, and attempts to manipulate, control, or punish. We may commit ourselves to helping, and then—when we discover our efforts are futile—succumb to anger or despair, or even back away. Meanwhile, the array of negative feelings we have just described only intensify the problem.

But it doesn't have to be that way.

Psychiatrist Gerald May, in writing about the healing of chemical addictions, describes the potential of the border network this way:

> For the addicted person alone, struggling with only willpower, the desire to continue the addiction will win. . . . [But] the caring community around the person has more potential than this. Even though this

> community is bound to have its own mind tricks and
> mixed motivations, it has a chance for a better per-
> spective. . . . Grace is always a present possibility for
> individuals, but its flow comes to fullness through
> community. [3]

As May points out, if for no other reason, people in
the border network have greater reserves of strength and
wisdom because they can draw from one another as they
reach out to the struggling person.

You don't have to suffer as the victim of another person's impulse control disorder. By cultivating healthy attitudes and strategies of your own toward that person,
you can maintain balance in your own life while actually
creating the opportunity for *the best possible chance of recovery.*

Freeing Yourself From the Search for a Magic Formula

Soon after Cherry and I began seeing Dr. Raymond
Vath, a psychotherapist in the Seattle area who specializes
in eating disorders, Dr. Vath challenged me with a star-
tling question: "Tell me, Dan," he asked, "do you really
believe you can control Cherry's behavior in an absolute
sense?"

I had to think long and hard before I could answer.
Certainly my experience up to that point had indicated
that, ultimately, I could not determine Cherry's diet—or
health. Only she could do that.

"I guess I could handcuff her, tie her to a chair, and
force-feed her," I finally answered, "but eventually the
time would come to set her free, and she would revert to
the same old behavior."

"That's right, Dan," said Dr. Vath. "The whole problem
of trying to extend absolute control over another member
of the human race is that, ultimately, it's quite impossible.
It's frustrating to the controller *and* to the one being controlled—an exercise in futility if the controlled individual

---

[3]Gerald G. May, M.D., *Addiction and Grace* (San Francisco: Harper and Row, 1988), p. 52.

doesn't choose to cooperate."

If there's any one lesson we learned in all the years fighting Cherry's compulsive disorder, it's that every human being possesses a free will. We simply cannot make other people's choices for them. In fact, our attempts to do so only lead to power struggles that actually *intensify an impulse control disorder.*

Having said that, we nevertheless believe that a number of insights from our experience and from Dr. Vath's wise counsel can help provide an environment for transformation in the life of the disordered person. People who live on the border of disorder are typically unaware of how deeply entangled they are in the problem and how much they contribute to it. Those who can learn some lessons from our experience and years of research will find that they can become a *therapeutic community* for the disordered person—and in the process they'll find their own spiritual growth accelerated as well. The healing experience can even become a reciprocal dynamic in which healing takes place for others in the network.

This book will help you learn how to give up your attempts to make the disordered person change and begin building the kind of supportive network required to begin the long process of healing. We should make it clear: You won't find a magic formula in these pages—this is not a "how-to" book with step-by-step instructions for "fixing" the disordered person. Each particular case is unique from all others, making a general formula impossible.

Even so, we can identify common factors contributing to the disorder, alerting you to signals, such as medical problems, low self-esteem, power struggles, and childhood trauma. Then you and the other members of the border network must sort them out.

To help you sift the clues, we will begin by providing a framework for understanding disordered behavior in general. This will help you understand its extreme and destructive forms, as well as the milder forms of disorders that most of us exhibit to one degree or another. Next, we will discuss typical means by which people attempt to cope with their problem as they first deny and then recognize it; rush to apply a "quick fix" to it; react in anger to the failure of the fix; and then try to bargain for a solution. Finally, we will examine the negative roles, including the problem of codependency, often played out in the border network, as well as positive, nurturing roles that contribute to healing.

This book primarily addresses situations that are not violent or otherwise immediately life-threatening. We recognize that extreme cases of that sort will require more radical and expert responses than those presented in most of these chapters. So we have devoted one chapter to identifying circumstances that require more serious measures such as professionally planned interventions, hospitalization, or disengagement from the family. We also explore how you can secure help and support for yourself. Above all, we don't want to give the false impression that you should allow a disorder to jeopardize the safety of anyone on the border while you are attempting to create a healing community.

Our hope is that as you come to appreciate just how great the challenge of overcoming an impulse control disorder is, you'll be able to take a more educated, realistic approach to the situation. Forewarned is forearmed—you'll know better how to tackle the emotional and relational crises of life on the border. And you'll find a new peace and freedom of your own as you become a part of the supportive network your loved one needs on the pilgrimage to recovery.

2

We're All in This Together

—Dan and Cherry

When the desert Christian monks of the ancient Middle East taught about humility, they wrote of an old holy man and his response when he saw another man sin. Weeping, the old man cried out: "He today; I tomorrow!"

That simple lament spoke to them powerfully of the broken human condition. By responding to another person's sin with a humble confession of his own weakness, the monk reminded us all how easily we fall, how dependent we are on grace, and how much we need forgiveness and repentance.

Compassion, Not Judgment

"He today; I tomorrow" is a declaration of our collective predicament. It has been written: "I have the desire to do what is good, but I cannot carry it out. For what I do is not the good I want to do; no, the evil I do not want to do—this I keep on doing."[1]

A more succinct description of the way impulse control sufferers feel cannot be found. They feel powerless to do the good they know to do, and equally powerless to stop doing what is wrong. But if the Scripture is, in fact, addressing here the problem of human sin in general—as the context of the passage indicates—then we must admit that impulse control disorders only represent one variety

---

[1]Romans 7:18b–19, NIV.

of the fallenness we all battle.

We may not all binge, abuse alcohol, or gamble. We may not starve ourselves until we become walking skeletons as some anorexics do, or engage in promiscuity. But we nevertheless do things we acknowledge to be inappropriate.

Most of us have made New Year's resolutions only to find they elude our grasp. We promise to lose weight, then gain five more pounds. We convince ourselves we'll keep a lid on credit card purchases, then run up a larger debt than ever.

Yet these are only the minor struggles. Much deeper and more serious are the disordered ways we have of dealing with others—ways that we know are wrong, and yet we persist. Our daily routines demonstrate that our professed values somehow seem unattainable. We spend countless hours watching television when we know we should be more present for our children. We make excuses for our professional failures when we realize we should acknowledge our accountability.

The major difference between us and the people with impulse control disorders is that we conveniently have a clinical term for their behavior. Theirs are active, aggressive disorders; ours are more a matter of neglect. Though some might argue that their disorders seem more dangerous than ours, often it is only a question of degree. And to one degree or another, we are all disordered. We all have "a hole in the soul" that demands to be filled. So each of us has chosen, consciously or otherwise, what we will put inside that hole for relief. We often try to fill that hole with things like sex, power, wealth, or drugs.

Our family's experience with anorexia and bulimia has made us much more sensitive to the "little" disorders that plague us all. At the same time Dan despaired about our eating disorder crisis, he was one who "pushed the envelope" riding his motorcycle. Adrenalin rushes made him feel high—living on the edge provided him an exhilaration he seemed to need. We have somehow joked about how he saw anorexia as one more challenge—an impossible case to crack.

Not Above . . . Beside

Why do we emphasize this point? Because we can't begin to appreciate the disordered person's predicament, or enter into the disordered struggle, unless we fully recognize our common ground. Until we see that no one is perfect, we will never find the common level ground called compassion. Instead, we will always be critical, judgmental, morally superior.

Sadly enough, the people in the border network—that group of people touched by the disordered person—are typically scandalized when they first encounter the problem behavior. They say in wonderment, "How could she act that way?" "He must know what he's doing is wrong." "Obviously they really don't want to stop."

Ironically, we have found this judgmental reaction to be pervasive in the evangelical Christian community—the very place where one would expect spiritual understanding for the human predicament. In fact, the voices of condemnation within that milieu appear to be even more shrill because of more rigid standards: "How could he possibly be a Christian and still be addicted?" "He's just being rebellious against God." "It's sin, pure and simple— why doesn't he just obey the Scripture?"

This type of reaction results from the elitist assumption that we have "arrived." It does little or nothing to help people with impulse control disorders. They will feel that "good" church folks are standing on a pulpit above them, casting stones. No wonder members of certain Christian movements are so reluctant to seek help in the church for their problems.

We need only consider a few simple questions to realize that we too are in a process toward wholeness and have not yet arrived. Take a minute to ask yourself:

- How loving and honorable are my thoughts?
- Would I want others to know my private fantasies?
- Would I like all of my personal ambitions exposed publicly?
- Would I want others to hear my unspoken thoughts of envy, jealousy or anger?

If we answer such questions honestly, we cannot remain in a position of superiority. We will place ourselves *alongside* rather than *above* the person who is struggling. In this way we will assume the posture of a healer rather than a judge. By humbly acknowledging our common plight, we take the first step toward becoming a part of a redemptive community that offers the optimum environment for recovery.

A Disordered Society

Even casual observation confirms that modern Western culture is itself disordered. The problem is apparent in dysfunctional families, materialistic values, manipulative media messages, racist business practices, bankrupt government policies, and criminal statistics.

Many of us tend to think of sin as purely an individual matter. But sin has, in fact, permeated human life at every level. Evil is not just individual, but also social, structural, systemic, and corporate.

As infants we all come home from the hospital to families with hurts, needs, prejudices, confused values, flawed social interaction, and learned behaviors carried forward from earlier generations as Eric Berne's[2] life script theory indicates. (We'll discuss this in chapter 3.) So we shouldn't be surprised that from the beginning we all have some spiritual and emotional hurdles to overcome.

Consider the destructive brew of emotions that would corrode the life of the teenage girl who recalled an event that happened after her father tragically died of a sudden heart attack:

> The night before the funeral, my grandmother lined up the children in the family and told us, "Now there are going to be people here tomorrow from all over the state. There will be straight backs and dry eyes. Do you understand?" That was the way our family operated. I was devastated, and for the first time I knew that feeling which other people have described

[2]Eric Berne, M.D., *What Do You Say After You Say Hello?* (New York: Grove Press, Inc., 1972).

as "nothing." There was no grief, no pain, just dead-
ness. I was nineteen. That lack of feeling went on for
months.[3]

When a family demands such an unhealthy response
to the emotional pain caused by a parent's death, children
are set up for emotional disaster. In this case, the teenager
soon became an alcoholic—as her father had been.

Even beyond the dents knocked into our souls by the
rough and tumble of family life, we are constantly hammered by media messages with warped values. Prime-
time "junk food" for the mind tells us that all problems
can be solved between the bed sheets or with a gun—all
within half an hour. Box office hits are filled with violence.
Songwriters pen sexually explicit lyrics. Teen magazines
are billboards depicting impossible standards of beauty
for their impressionable young readers. And self-help
books tell us how to get rich and manipulate others.

Of course we cannot simply blame our personal problems on social conditions. But neither can we deny that
our disordered culture has contributed to the mess. Our
culture has a deep poverty of spirit, and our lack of spiritual grounding has helped drive us to pain and despair.
As Pope John Paul II has noted, "All of us experience first-
hand the sad effects of blind submission to pure consum-
erism: in the first place a crass materialism, and at the
same time a *radical dissatisfaction*, because one quickly
learns . . . that the more one possesses the more one
wants, while deeper aspirations remain unsatisfied and
perhaps even stifled."[4]

The result is a vast field of human wreckage. Dr. Ron-
ald J. Dougherty of the Benjamin Rush Center in Syra-
cuse, New York, notes soberly: "I'm frightened for the
American public. It took about fifty years to get to ten
million alcoholics in this country, but only *four years* to get
four million coke [that is, cocaine] addicts."[5]

Our friend, Dr. Raymond Vath, has noted the effects

---

[3]Rachel V., *A Woman Like You: Life Stories of Women Recovering from Alcoholism and Addiction* (San Francisco: Harper & Row, 1985), p. 4.
[4]Pope John Paul II, "On Social Concern," Encyclical letter, Dec. 30, 1987.
[5]Quoted in Ed Storti and Janet Keller, *Crisis Intervention: Acting Against
Addiction* (New York: Crown Publishers, 1988), p. 1.

of destructive media messages on our emotional and even physical health:

> We must challenge the false illusions about life as presented by television, movies and the popular press. . . . When television heroes engage in promiscuous sex and never catch herpes or AIDS, viewers are being deceived. When drugs and alcohol are glamorized but liver disease or brain atrophy are never mentioned, we, the public, are being seduced into false beliefs.[6]

Or take a simple example close to home for our family: The image of the "perfect" female figure as portrayed in the media has become thinner in recent years. Look at statues from earlier periods, such as the Venus de Milo, and you'll see that, historically, the ideal woman would look overweight next to most women on the covers of fashion magazines and in movies today. One study of statistics from the Metropolitan Life Insurance tables shows that between 1970 and 1978, just over five percent of female life insurance policyholders between the ages of twenty and twenty-nine were as slim as the average Miss America pageant contestants. Considering that these contestants are much more full-figured than most of the models employed by the fashion industry, we can see how few women actually fit that emaciated and yet supposedly ideal shape.[7]

Who can doubt that this intimidating message to American women has contributed significantly to the rising number of anorexics and bulimics in our country? The statistics are frightening: A recent nationwide study of American high school students by the federal Centers for Disease Control in Atlanta shows that fully half of the girls surveyed were trying to lose weight whether they needed to or not. Half said they skip meals, a fifth use diet pills, and about 14 percent make themselves vomit to lose weight.

[6]Raymond E. Vath, M.D., *Counseling Those With Eating Disorders* (Waco, Tex.: Word, 1986), p. 139.
[7]D.M. Garner, P.E. Garfinkel, D. Schwartz and M. Thompson, "Cultural Expectations of Thinness in Women," *Psychological Reports* 47 (1980), pp. 483–491.

Although previous studies have concluded that one in five American teenagers is overweight, one in three girls said she felt she was "fat," compared with only about 15 percent of the boys. The result: Anorexia affects about 1 percent of the nation's teenage girls and has the highest death rate among that group of any psychiatric disorder. In addition, about 3 percent of teenage girls nationwide suffer from bulimia.

For Cherry, the constant pressure from the media's emphasis on thinness was a double-barreled threat. Like other American women, she was constantly confronted by Hollywood with an unrealistic standard of beauty. But worse yet, as a member of an entertainment family who frequently appeared on television, she found herself on stage around women bound by that standard, and the image of her own body was being held up for scrutiny by viewers all over the nation.

It's tough enough when media messages tell us we need a certain car or vacation that is beyond our financial means. Even then, if we buy into the message, we can promise ourselves that someday we'll be able to afford the item. But how much worse it is when Madison Avenue or Hollywood subtly tells us we ought to *look* a certain way—an appearance impossible to attain.

For most of us, our genes have already determined that we'll never quite meet minimum media standards for beauty. Yet we may nevertheless spend a lifetime in a futile attempt to overcome our genetic program. Like an oak tree striving to be a willow, we can't possibly succeed. We all sense the inescapable pressure of such fraudulent media messages.

Again, we don't wish to fix blame on others for our personal problems. We simply want you to recognize that the healing process may not be as easy as we presumed— that overcoming a lifetime of subjection to deeply ingrained, warped messages may take a more calculated, process-oriented approach to produce true liberation from destructive behavior.

Fearfully and Wonderfully Made

Border people typically ask one insistent question when they discover a person's disorder: Why? Why would someone who seems reasonable and considerate engage in a behavior that is so obviously self-destructive and ultimately harmful to others?

We'll probably never know the full answer to that question. Perhaps that is what is meant by "the *mystery* of iniquity"[8] Who can say exactly why we choose options that obviously carry such negative consequences?

The mystery of sin is hidden within the labyrinth of the human soul, whose dark, convoluted passageways of perception and memory, motive and response lead in a thousand directions. Consider for a moment that, according to psychologists, every sense impression we have ever received since birth—sights, sounds, smells, tastes, touches—are permanently registered in our memory. Though we can't recall them all at will, they nevertheless exist in the depths of our memories, each one exerting some influence, however infinitesimal, on our behavior. As one psychologist put it, nothing we experience is ever genuinely repressed; it's only disguised. Behavior disorders are sometimes disguises for painful things we would rather forget.

No wonder, then, that the psalmist wrote that we are "fearfully and wonderfully made . . . curiously wrought" beings.[9] The complexity of the human soul makes possible both its remarkable creativity and its astounding ability to attain uniqueness among billions of other creatures. Before the beauty of such a creation, we must stand in awe—without the pretense that we can somehow identify and measure every factor involved in a particular behavior.

In that light, we see the shallowness of statements often heard from the border that attempt a simplistic explanation for a disorder. In one letter Cherry received, a young anorexic girl reported: "My father has threatened to put me in the hospital if I don't put on weight. He says I am just trying to get attention, and if attention is what I want, he can arrange it with doctors who will force-feed me."

---

[8]2 Thessalonians 2:7, KJV, emphasis added.
[9]Psalm 139:14, 15, KJV.

We only diminish the chances for recovery when we take an approach like this, reducing the process of healing to changing behavior—and in a forced way at that. A complex disorder like anorexia cannot be explained—much less treated—as a simple play for attention, though that motive may indeed be one factor among many. To become an active member of a therapeutic community, we must humbly admit the limits of our understanding and abandon attempts to find a single causative factor that can easily be "fixed."

The Strict Sin Model of Disordered Behavior

Though we can't fully comprehend all the contributing factors to human behavior, we can nevertheless understand a great deal about the dynamics of particular disorders, and what we do know can contribute to recovery. In general, three basic models have been offered by theologians and scientists to account for disordered behavior. The first two, commonly held today, underlie the often heated debate within some circles over the appropriateness of seeking help from mental health professionals. The third model, we believe, moves beyond the limited parameters of that debate to offer a more accurate and hopeful alternative for understanding and treating impulse control disorders.

The first model, and the oldest, we might call a *strict sin model*. In its earliest pagan form, this explanation for disordered behavior, and for physical illness as well, claimed that moral failure alone was the culprit. Whether people suffered from obsessive fears or the black plague, they suffered—they reasoned—because they had offended the gods, and the gods were visiting their wrath upon them. The remedy was to go see a priest, let him discern the sin, and then offer whatever sacrifices he prescribed.[10]

This model has survived in a modified form in certain

---

[10]F. Kraupl Taylor, *The Concepts of Illness, Disease and Morbus* (Cambridge, England: Cambridge University Press).

circles of the Jewish and Christian traditions even today. People with impulse control disorders, for example, are often told that their problem is a simple matter of rebellion against God. If they will simply repent of their sin, they will be fine. Meanwhile, they're often expected to undergo a degree of suffering in the process—the equivalent of the pagan sacrifice to appease the gods.

Even in contemporary secular approaches to mental health care, a version of this model can be found, though it doesn't use the term "sin." In this type of therapy, people with impulse control disorders are viewed simply as bad people making bad choices who need to be guided into better decisions. If the disorder is dangerous enough, such as alcoholism or drug addiction, then they are helped to overcome the behavior with threats of harsh consequences if they do not reform.

Whether in its religious or secular form, the strict sin model assumes that disordered people are totally responsible for their own behavior, regardless of contributing factors. It assumes that they can always freely choose by a simple act of the will to avoid destructive habits. In this model, then, the "blame" for an impulse control disorder lies squarely with the disordered person.

The Strict Sickness Model

The second model of behavioral disorder might be called the *strict sickness* model. According to this explanation, mental health problems are simply natural processes with resultant causes, usually with a traumatic or a biological basis. Thus, impulse control disorders have nothing to do with individual choice.

In opposition to the strict sin model, the strict sickness model says that disordered people are "patients" who are not responsible for their "illness." If there's any blame to be placed, it is usually centered on the patient's environment or parents—though to follow through with this model logically, the parents would have to be innocent victims themselves of someone else. Since disorders are sicknesses, it becomes the doctor's job to make the patients better. If they just follow medical or therapy directives, they will recover.

The problem with these two models, simply stated, is that in most cases of behavioral disorders, therapy based solely on these explanations is not adequate.

No doubt researchers have discovered that some behavioral disorders have a biological basis, or at least a biological component; these must be treated accordingly by a doctor's prescription. We can be thankful for mood-stabilizing medications that counteract biochemical imbalances in many people suffering from depression, hyperactivity, and similar problems. But for many disorders, medication, though necessary, is simply not enough to effect a cure.

We also know that trauma contributes to many disorders. The teenage girl whose story we quoted earlier, who was forbidden by her grandmother to cry when her father died, had already endured her share of emotional injury. As a five-year-old, she had had a temper tantrum one day when her parents announced they were going out for the evening. The child hit her mother and told her she hated her and wished she would die. The parents went on with their plans, but the mother died in a terrible auto accident that night, never to come home again.

The little girl believed that her "wish" had killed her mother. Now an adult alcoholic, she sees her drinking as a way of anesthetizing the guilt and loneliness she has felt ever since that terrible night.[11]

Sixty percent of people with eating disorders have been sexually abused. Often the disorder is triggered by an event such as the termination of a romantic relationship. But not all people who are molested or jilted develop an eating disorder, so we cannot conclude that the "trigger" event is the single *cause* of the problem. Multiple factors must be present for the disorder to develop. Meanwhile, fixing blame on a person—or event—does little to bring about recovery.

Thus the strict sickness model isn't sufficiently com-

---

[11]Rachel V., comp., *Women Like You* (San Francisco: Harper & Row, 1985), pp. 1-2.

prehensive to address the situation. But neither is the strict sin model. It's certainly true that human beings have free will and are responsible for many of their choices. Yet the strict sin model doesn't take into consideration the mysterious depths of the human soul or the complexity of physiological realities discussed earlier. Many behavioral disorders have components that transcend simple choice. Biochemical deficiencies, childhood trauma, parental modeling, the power of habit, and cultural reinforcers all contribute to behaviors resistant to change by sheer willpower alone.

We should note here that the debate over the cause and cure of disordered behavior has often been sidetracked by oversimplification. The degree to which those who are disordered are responsible for their behavior is argued widely. It is a debate, however, that thus far has proven futile.

The Adaptive Model

We believe that a third model of behavior—the *adaptive* model—makes more sense than the other two. According to this approach, disorders result when our ability to cope with the stresses of life is somehow overwhelmed. In the process of attempting to cope with pain or other problems, we choose to respond in different ways. Some responses are adaptive; that is, they work. Some, however, are maladaptive; they simply don't work.

According to Dr. Harry Croft, addictive behavior attempts in a maladaptive way to accomplish five purposes. It helps people:

1. avoid dealing constructively with *time*;
2. avoid dealing with *difficult feelings* (fear, anger, bitterness, self-hatred);
3. avoid dealing constructively with a *negative self-image*;
4. avoid dealing realistically with *relationship issues*.
5. avoid dealing effectively with *stress and stressors*.[12]

---

[12]From private correspondence between Dr. Harry Croft and Cherry, November 19, 1987.

A recurring theme in cases of addiction, for example, is that the addict is anesthetizing some emotional pain. It may be grief, rage or low self-esteem; it may be pain resulting from childhood incest, gender confusion or financial hopelessness. The disordered person is attempting to deaden the pain.

One alcoholic described it this way:

> What alcohol did for me was distance me from all my feelings of anxiety and despair and feeling so separate from everyone else. It put me on the other side of those feelings, and it made it possible to act as if I were really more comfortable than I really was. Alcohol became my problem solver for feelings.

For her, the sense of comfort and protection from alcohol was "palpable." The bottle provided, as she called it, "a zone of anesthesia."[13]

An alcoholic who drinks to bury wounds this way may be making an understandable effort to cope. But the choice is nonetheless maladaptive. It doesn't work because it only deadens pain temporarily, and it ultimately generates more pain than it alleviates.

The anorexic behavior of many young girls, to take another example, results at least in part from their attempts to cope with their own feelings of powerlessness. They feel dominated by people around them—usually men, such as a father or husband—who exert excessive levels of control over their personal lives. So they try to cope with the problem by establishing control over one very important area of their lives: food. The disorder is, in part, their maladaptive attempt to overcome powerlessness.

These examples help us to appreciate how the adaptive model takes into account the complexity of human nature. It suggests that behavioral disorder is in some sense chosen, so we bear a degree of responsibility for it, and it cannot be healed without our cooperation. Yet it also recognizes that our choices can draw us into such binds that we cannot escape alone. We need more than pure will-

---

[13]Rachel V., p. 67.

power; we need help from others who can compassion-
ately illuminate the problem and support us as we embark
upon our journey toward health.

The predicament may be described this way: It is possible to dig a pit by yourself that's too deep to climb out
of by yourself. In response to stress we can make maladaptive choices that put us deeper and deeper into a psychological "hole"—a hole so deep we cannot escape without assistance. Though we certainly bear some
responsibility for our dilemma, we can't simply choose to
rescue ourselves.

Why Use the Term *Disorder*?

You can see now why we've chosen the term *disorder*
to describe the problems we're dealing with. Simply labeling the behavior itself *sin* would be inaccurate. Much
of the disordered person's behavior is an understandable
yet misguided attempt to cope with life, not an intentional
act of rebellion.

On the other hand, we've avoided the word *sickness*
and its accompanying terms, *patient* and *victim*, because
these labels are also deficient. The disordered person may,
in fact, have a physical malady or be the victim of trauma
inflicted by another. But using these words paints a picture of passivity and helplessness that fails to fully reflect
the person's struggle. This undermines both responsibility
and hope.

Consequently, we speak instead of a *disorder*. This
word, we believe, more accurately describes the problem
without assigning blame the way *sin* does or denying the
role of choices the way *sickness* does. It simply states that
the life of the human struggler has gotten "out of order":
values have been confused, priorities have been inverted,
motives have been convoluted, desires have been discon-
nected from their appropriate means of fulfillment.

The term also has a rich history of theological thought.
Some of the greatest teachers of the Church in earlier
generations referred to human fallenness as disorder.
Catherine of Siena, the great fourteenth-century Italian
theologian, wrote often of "the disordered will," "disor-

dered passions," "disordered fear," and especially "disordered love."

From Catherine's perspective, normal human responses to life, like fear and love, can become attached to the wrong objects or twisted in the wrong directions. The result is destructive behavior—acting out of the confusion of a soul whose very structure is tangled and dislocated.

Her diagnosis shows us that people who ask why anorexics don't have the willpower to control their problem are overlooking an obvious fact insightfully pointed out once by Cherry's father, Pat Boone: "It takes tremendous willpower to starve yourself when you're surrounded by an abundance of food." The anorexic doesn't lack *willpower*; rather, the will is *disordered*, so its power is being exerted in the wrong direction.

Catherine agreed that disorders are developed in part through people's free choice of wrong responses to situations encountered in life. She also concurred, however, that once people are trapped in a "disordered life," they can't break out of it alone. To use her striking, powerful image, we can say that by their own maladaptive choices, disordered people have "encrusted their heart in a diamond rock" that they themselves are powerless to shatter.[14]

How, then, does the disordered person break out of the "rock"? How does that person climb out of the pit? The next chapter will introduce three therapeutic approaches growing out of the adaptive model that offer what we believe is the best chance for recovery. To succeed, however, these therapies need the participation of the people who live in that sometimes frightening and precarious place—the border of disorder.

---

[14]Catherine of Siena, *The Dialogue* (New York: Paulist Press, 1980), pp. 31, 32, 61, 73, 77, 91.

3

The Healing Trio: Medical, Cognitive, and Relational Therapies

—Dan and Cherry

Not long ago the news media reported that a well-known TV evangelist had been exposed in a morally compromising situation—for the second time. The first incident had been followed by a public confession and an expression of repentance. Many felt satisfied that the leader was taking the right course for correction. But following the second incident we can see that merely admitting to sin failed to rectify the disordered behavior.

This time, many people who subscribe to the strict sin model philosophy have written the man off, declaring that his public career is over. On the other hand, some therapists analyzing the incident have suggested that the man is struggling with a form of sexual addiction and requires professional help, not condemnation, to recover. Though many conservative, evangelical Christians denounce or distrust psychology, incidents such as this suggest that along with repentance, therapy may well be necessary for wholeness.

Beyond the Sin vs. Sickness Debate

This unseemly public scandal illustrates the dilemma of many who have an impulse control disorder or who want to help someone who does. They have been taught that they can choose to "behave" themselves by simple repentance and exertion of willpower, and they have been bombarded with religious propaganda that seems to support a strict sin model. Yet many find that mere willingness to obey has not provided them with a means of escape from their destructive behaviors.

We are personally aware of many such situations, and must assume there are countless more. We knew, for instance, a church counselor whose sexual addiction led him to have sex with several of his female counselees. A local pastor once confessed to us that he retreated from his high-stress work every afternoon with a joint of marijuana. We are acquainted with a religious education instructor who has long been addicted to diet pills. And we personally know a missionary who was discovered to have a reoccurring problem with pornography.

Many secular mental health professionals refuse to discuss sin at all, which has contributed to some Christians' aversion to professional care. Just recently, for example, a book by a Christian medical doctor has appeared lambasting the sickness model of impulse control disorders as spiritually bankrupt. Sadly enough, however, he offered in its place the equally deficient sin model without recognizing that a third, more complex understanding of reality might be possible. Failure to transcend the limited terms of the sin vs. sickness debate will, tragically, keep helpful therapeutic strategies beyond the reach of desperate, disordered people.

We feel it's important to remind readers that in our personal experience we have frequently encountered church-oriented people who, because of a religious collective unconscious attitude, feel that it is a sign of weakness or defeat to engage in the use of medicines or psychotherapy, particularly if the medical expertise is not church-related or "biblically based." We agree with Christians who have recognized that some approaches to psychology, like B.F. Skinner's behavioral determinism, do in fact run counter to the biblical teaching about human freedom and responsibility. But we regret that the conservative Christian community has tended to let the misguided efforts of a few psychological schools discredit the whole idea of therapeutic care. In the final analysis, truth is truth, wherever we may find it.

Psychological researchers have discovered, for example, that certain addictive behaviors lead to an immediate reduction of physical tension in the disordered person. That bit of knowledge can help us understand how such a short-term benefit might make an otherwise destructive habit seem worthwhile. The fact that the insight may have come from a secular researcher should not rule out our appropriation of it any more than we should throw away all cookbooks and auto repair manuals simply because they weren't written by Christian cooks and mechanics. How many of us would prefer to fly with an inexperienced Christian pilot over a non-Christian, commercially-licensed expert? We would venture to say, no one.

Mood-Stabilizing Medications

Perhaps the sharpest debate about therapy in some areas of the Christian community rages over the prescription of mood-stabilizing medications for depression, hyperactivity, and other problems. This issue is of special importance in treating impulse control disorders because so many of these disorders appear to be depression-driven. Such medications as lithium carbonate, a mineral salt, often bring immediate and dramatic results in the treatment of manic depression, clearing away a major obstacle in the treatment of destructive behaviors. Thus the first element in the healing trio of treatment is typically *medical therapy*.

Studies have demonstrated, for example, that bulimia is positively managed in about ninety percent of cases by antidepressant medication. Other research indicates that a group of alcoholics placed on lithium carbonate and released from a detoxification program experienced a significantly reduced rate of relapse.[1]

---

[1]H. Pope, J. Hudson and J. Jonas, "Bulimia Treated With Imipramine: A Placebo Controlled, Double Blind Study," *American Journal of Psychiatry* 140, 1983; pp. 554–558, 1983; T. Walsh, J. Stewart, S. Roose, M. Gladis and A. Glassman, "Treatment of Bulimia With Phenelzine: A Placebo Controlled, Double-Blind Study," *Archives of General Psychiatry* 41, 1984; pp. 1105–1109; R. Horne, "Buproprion in the Treatment of Bulimia," unpublished; cited in Raymond E. Vath, M.D., *Counseling Those With Eating Disorders* (Waco, Tex.: Word, 1986), p. 206.

We appreciate the healthy suspicion of drugs that many people have. Perhaps they have observed people addicted to medications such as diet pills, compounding the problem. They may also fear that treating the symptoms of depression without addressing its root causes is doomed to failure, like treating appendicitis with aspirin.

The point to be made here, of course, is that frequently the root cause of depression is a *biological* one. When this is the case, medication is not an attempt to cover the symptoms, as if the person's mood were being artificially elevated by a drug while the real problem is being ignored. Instead, the medication actually corrects a biochemical disorder in the body that affects the brain. The problem may stem, for example, from a defect in the thyroid gland, or from insufficient transmitter substances required by brain cells to relay information.

Given this information, mood-stabilizing medication should be accepted as a component of therapy for many impulse control disorders just as readily as we accept insulin in the treatment of diabetes. The realization that many behavioral problems have a biological component should also make those of us on the border of disorder more understanding and less judgmental toward people who struggle. One result of Cherry's experience, in fact, was that years later we could be more understanding when our son was diagnosed as hyperactive, and less reluctant to apply drug therapy.

We know a leader of a large parachurch ministry who was diagnosed as a manic-depressive and went out of town secretly for treatment. He was put on lithium carbonate, and his therapy has been successful. But to this day most of his staff and friends are unaware he is on medication because he's too ashamed to let them know. Sadly enough, until the conservative Christian community changes its attitudes toward medication, most of those who use it will conclude as he has that they must remain in the closet to avoid scandal, rejection and isolation.

Cognitive Therapy

Medication is often necessary for treating behavioral disorders, but medicine is rarely a comprehensive solution. One study of bulimics showed, for example, that antidepressant medicines helped considerably in the short term. But by themselves, these medications weren't enough to keep the bulimics from returning to their behavior in the long run.

A second ingredient is necessary in a successful therapy for impulse control disorders: *cognitive therapy*. In cognitive therapy, the therapist clarifies the disordered person's choices and the outcome of those choices.

Cognitive therapy provides an effective tool for behavioral change because knowledge is power. Disordered people have little chance of recovery if they don't understand the dynamics of their problem. They must be taught the factors that have contributed to a disorder's development, the current reinforcers that contribute to its maintenance, and the resulting consequences if it continues.

The complexity of human beings that we described earlier confounds us not only when we try to understand another person's behavior, but also when we try to analyze our own. Obviously, no person can ever fully plumb the depths of another person's being. But perhaps less obvious is the truth that we can't explore very deeply into our own depths if we make the journey alone.

When a friend comes to us and says he wants to stop drinking, yet goes out a few hours later and drinks, we believe that in those moments of confession he has been sincere, and that he really wants to stop. The problem, however, is that *he wants to do something that he simply doesn't know how to do.* Of course, he knows how to pick up a glass or put it down. But he doesn't understand the interior forces motivating him, binding him, and undermining his intention to stop.

That is why people with behavioral problems need help from professionals who have had training and experience in recognizing the common factors in impulse control disorders. The therapist may not be able to tell them everything that lies inside them, but can usually provide enough pieces of the puzzle to help them initiate the healing process.

Cherry still remembers, for example, the powerful impact of a simple question Dr. Vath asked her one day soon after she'd begun seeing him for help. "Tell me, Cherry," he said. "Why is it that you want to die?"

"I don't really think I *do*," she answered.

"Well," he said, "it appears from your behavior that you do. You see, anorexia nervosa may be seen as a slow form of suicide."

Cherry had never seen her condition as suicidal before, but she couldn't escape the reality of Dr. Vath's observation. Whether or not she wanted to admit it, she was gradually killing herself, draining her life away ounce by ounce.

That kind of insight, gleaned by a therapist from years of training and experience, can "turn on the light" inside a disordered person's head. In this case, the connection between anorexia and a death wish opened doors for Cherry to explore why it was that she hated herself so deeply—and how she could begin to love herself instead.

Clinical psychologist Lawrence Crabb illustrates the importance of cognitive therapy with the example of a Christian man who is compulsively driven to make money. The man needs to feel significant, as we all do, and is motivated to meet that need somehow. A false value system has taught him that in order to be important he must have money. So his, perhaps unconscious, goal becomes making as much money as possible.

At the same time, this man has heard it said that the root of all evil is the love of money, and he fully agrees with that biblical insight. Yet he still feels an inner compulsion to make money. A repentant attitude makes him feel better temporarily, but his drive to possess and accumulate wealth remains strong. Crabb concludes (speaking in the first person of the compulsive money-maker):

> My real problem is not a love of money but rather a wrong belief, a learned assumption that personal significance depends on having money. *Until that idea is deliberately and consciously rejected, I will always want money*, no matter how many times I confess to God my sin of wanting money.[2]

---

[2]Lawrence J. Crabb, Jr., *Inside Out* (Grand Rapids, Mich.: Zondervan, 1977), p. 77; emphasis is original to the text.

If a counselor or therapist can help such a person uncover the hidden assumption about how to have the need
for significance met, that person will begin the process
leading to freedom.

Life Scripts

Some of the most important insights we gained from
therapy grew out of the notion of "life scripts," developed
by Eric Berne, M.D., in his book *What Do You Say After
You Say Hello?*[3] Dr. Vath used this concept to help us see
that each one of us is handed a script by our parents that
we tend to act out, whether or not we're aware of it. With
remarkable consistency, people seem to repeat the same
basic plot lived by their parents, because modeling by parents or other significant adults is the most powerful behavioral determinant in the life of children.

For some people the script is largely positive. But most
of us are aware of at least a few things in the lives of our
parents that we would just as soon avoid. One task of the
therapist, then, is to help the disordered person recognize
where a life script may be contributing to disordered behavior so that part of the script can be, so to speak, re-
written.

This is not to say, of course, that parents are therefore
to be *blamed* for their child's disorder. As we noted before,
blaming doesn't really help to solve the problem. When
the parents of young anorexics ask us what they did
wrong, we simply reply that exploring the question is usually unproductive. There are no perfect parents.

If we did decide to assign the blame to the parents,
then what would we do about it? Punish them? Placing
blame does not contribute toward healing.

Instead, we must ask, What is the problem and what
are the solutions? What is the disordered person doing,
and what happens when he or she does it? We examine
the cause to understand the effect. If we can understand
the truth about this disorder, the truth will free us from

---

[3]Eric Berne, M.D., *What Do You Say After You Say Hello?* (New York: Grove
Press, 1972).

it. Self-knowledge will bring the disordered person the power to change.

For people in the border network as well, such knowledge brings power: power to forgive, to be patient, to support and encourage without condemnation. The more border people know about the *causes* of the disorder, the better position they are in to become a healing community.

Disorder Reinforcers

The same is true when it comes to understanding the factors that contribute to the *maintenance* of a disorder. Life scripts from the early years may have set the stage for a maladaptive response; but therapists and others must also help the disordered person recognize how wrong choices are *reinforced*.

One way maladaptive choices made in our childhood are strengthened into adulthood is simply through *the power of habit*. We could well rewrite the proverb about child rearing (Prov. 22:6) this way: "Train up a child in the way he should go, and when he is old, he'll have a terrible time changing it!"

All of us as children learned some maladaptive behaviors because our parents were neither perfect nor perfectly wise. The wrong responses to life we learn in our youth are now difficult to change after years of repetition. Their grooves run deep in our minds.

Of course, habit is actually a good thing in itself; we don't have to relearn every morning all that we've ever been taught. But repetition's power to reinforce a pattern of behavior can work against us as well, so we have to replace bad habits with good ones. When the entrenched behavior is a serious disorder, that difficult task calls for the help of those around us—the border network.

Disorders can be reinforced as well by people who repeat the scripts our parents handed us. Often we marry someone much like our parent of the opposite sex. If we had problems in our relationship with that parent, the same conflict is quite likely to occur in our marriage.

Women who grew up with domineering fathers, for example, tend to marry domineering men. If such a woman has an impulse control disorder with a power struggle operating at the center—as it often does—then the disorder receives strong encouragement to continue. An authoritarian employer can also add to the problem. Thus members of the border network may themselves be unwittingly reinforcing the disorder.

Perhaps the most powerful reinforcers of maladaptive choices are found in the messages we receive from our culture. As we noted before, when a society is itself disordered, its values can have a warping effect on our own. Distorted ways of viewing ourselves and others permeate our daily lives—television, periodicals, books, radio, films, billboards—all the more powerful because of the subtlety of the message. The pervasive and relentless pressure of these destructive values nearly guarantees that we will absorb them to one extent or another.

For anorexics, the message from Madison Avenue is "Look thin or be rejected." For sexual addicts, the word from Hollywood is "Happiness is impossible without promiscuity." For compulsive liars, daily news headlines about unscrupulous politicians and business people point toward one conclusion: "Integrity doesn't pay."

How do we counteract the pressure of those inappropriate messages? The insights of a therapist can show them for what they are—dangerous lies. But with the culture's "siren song" constantly in our ears, the disordered person needs a chorus of positive voices to sing louder still.

That's precisely why the border network is so critical to the recovery process. Family and friends, the pastor and doctor, even an employer can take on the role of *positive reinforcer*—people who "bear witness" to the truth in the life of the person struggling to be freed by the truth. By their words, attitudes and behaviors, they can model an alternative to the destructive life scripts and cultural values that have been inherited and absorbed by the disordered person.

Low Self-Esteem

Cognitive therapy, we've said, is based on the reality that knowledge is power. But knowledge is not enough.

Nearly every day we meet people who know they're choosing misery and death even though they recognize an alternative is available.

Why don't people always choose what they know to be for their own good? Human motives, as we noted, are often too tangled to unknot thoroughly. But at the heart of perhaps most impulse control disorders lies a single problem that accounts for behavior that is knowingly self-destructive: *low self-esteem*.

Self-esteem enters the disordered picture in at least two ways. First, life experiences of the past may have damaged a person's sense of personal worth. Somewhere along the line, someone has convinced the disordered person that he or she is "bad" and unworthy of love. Most likely it was a parent or other significant adult—perhaps another relative or teacher—in the person's childhood, though it may have been peers instead.

The message may have been explicit, through such repeated statements as "You're a bad girl"; "You're just stupid"; "You'll never amount to anything." But the message of rejection may have taken a nonverbal vehicle as well: emotional distance, physical absence, abandonment, violence, sexual abuse. Whatever the case, the message is the same: *"You're worthless!"*

The sense of rejection can be heightened if we have a perfectionist streak in our temperament, or if circumstances seem to confirm the message. Perhaps good grades in school evade us. Maybe we have trouble getting dates in the teen years. Our physical features may well fail to match our culture's standards of beauty. Or we may end up in a low-paying, dead-end job.

Yet low self-esteem is not only a deep *root* of disorders. It also is a *result* of disorders. Psychiatrist Gerald May observes:

> Addiction splits the will in two, one part desiring freedom and the other desiring only to continue the addictive behavior. This internal inconsistency begins to erode self-esteem. How much can I respect myself if I do not know even what I really want?

May adds that even worse damage to self-esteem results from the disordered person's repeated failures at trying to overcome the problem. In modern Western society, these failures are viewed as especially demeaning because we have come to see ourselves as objects of our own creation. "When we fail at managing ourselves," May concludes, "we feel defective."[4]

In recent years the nature and consequences of low self-esteem have been widely examined in published materials. Our purpose here is not to deal with the issue comprehensively; other writers have done that job well. We do need to note, however, that nurturing a healthy sense of self-worth must be an element in any successful treatment of an impulse control disorder. Not surprisingly, the border network is critical to that task.

The therapist can say to the disordered person, "If you keep abusing drugs, it will kill you." But at some level the disordered person may well reply, "That's exactly what I intend to happen."

When the therapist pursues the next obvious line of questioning, as Dr. Vath did with Cherry—"Why do you want to die?"—sooner or later a disturbing answer emerges, in one form or another: *"I'm bad and I deserve to die."* Self-destructive behavior is most often a form of self-punishment.

The result: Our "sins" must be punished, so we punish ourselves. If we make a mistake, we beat up on ourselves instead of solving the problem. And if in coping with the pain of rejection our maladaptive choices entrap us in an impulse control disorder, we may, in effect, be prescribing the death penalty for ourselves.

Love in Earthen Vessels

How do we escape that penalty? By overcoming our self-hatred. How do we learn to love ourselves instead? We must come to accept that we were created by a benevolent God who loves each one of us. To accept and rest in the fact that we are created by a loving, all-powerful

---

[4]Gerald G. May, M.D., *Addiction and Grace* (San Francisco: Harper & Row, 1988), p. 42.

God—this is a critical foundation stone of cognitive therapy. If the therapist isn't a Christian, then those in the border network must communicate the assurances of love to the disordered person.

And here is the most important step: We must *ourselves* love that person with acceptance and unending patience. The original message of personal worthlessness was demonstrated to him or her by human beings. *The new message of personal worth must be demonstrated by other human beings as well.*

Simplistic directives, even passages quoted from the Bible (however true they may be), are not enough. At its deepest levels, a wounded soul needs more emotionally convincing evidence that he or she is truly loved. And this calls for a consistent demonstration of love from other human beings.

All this is to say, after all, that divinity often chooses to work through human vessels. No doubt we are "earthen vessels," as the Bible says (2 Cor. 4:7, KJV), but we can be vessels of healing love nonetheless. The Christian faith is an incarnational faith: We believe that the natural, the physical, the ordinary is invested by God with the supernatural, the spiritual, the extraordinary—if we are available to it. We are "sacraments" to one another because we encounter love and healing power through one another.

The Power of Relational Therapy

Let's consider the powerful healing potential of the border network. Here are the people who mean the most to the disordered person, whose approval that person most desperately wants, whose words and nonverbal communications the person is most likely to believe. Relationships in the network may have been strained or even broken by the disorder; the "earthquake zone" around the epicenter may be strewn with the rubble of anger, fear, and confusion. Nevertheless, here, within the border network, lies the unequaled opportunity to share deep, lasting healing to the disordered person. Healing moments suddenly present themselves for us to become living sacraments of love.

In short: If you can love a disordered person, you yourself can be that person's best therapy. You may not have professional training; you may even feel that your supply of love has nearly been exhausted. Nevertheless, your relationship with the disordered person can become a living channel of healing. That is the meaning of *relational therapy*—that transcendent, personal third element in the healing trio.

But what does it mean in practical terms to show love? The definition of love we have found to be most helpful comes from Harry Stack Sullivan, a psychiatrist who taught that *love is a condition that exists when another person's well-being and security are as important to you as your own.*[5] With that definition in mind, the rest of this book will examine some concrete ways in which the border network can literally love the disordered person back to health— and life. Though we have no formulas to offer, we believe that some of our personal experiences can at least demonstrate how genuine caring strategies might be hammered out in the admittedly difficult circumstances surrounding an impulse control disorder.

In particular, we have found that healing love requires an atmosphere of honesty and empathy. The critical role of honesty will emerge in chapter 5. There we will discuss the damaging effects of denial and deceit that perpetuate and intensify a disorder.

Empathy allows us to think and feel what the hurting person thinks and feels, to see as that person sees, to hear as that person hears, to experience true compassion. The understanding that comes from empathy is the foundation for healing. In fact, some provocative studies of colicky babies and severe arthritic sufferers even suggest that trained, professional "empathizers"—who attempted to feel in themselves the discomfort of the patients—were able to reduce the pain of those suffering. Later X-rays

---

[5]Harry Stack Sullivan, *Conceptions of Modern Psychiatry* (New York: W.W. Norton & Co., 1953), pp. 42–43.

even showed a measurable decalcification of the arthritic joints![6]

If empathy has that much power to heal, then people in the border network need to gain some sense of what it's like to wrestle with an impulse control disorder from the perspective of the disordered person. For that reason, Cherry will tell us her story in the next chapter. From her painfully honest account, you can learn about the internal struggles that led to her anorexia and bulimia, the various ways in which she tried to cope with it, and how she perceived the efforts of the people who, in time, helped love her back to life and health.

[6]"Natural Processes of Healing," Roche Labs, Division of Hoffman-La Roche, Inc., Nutley, NJ 07110 as cited in Raymond E. Vath, M.D. and Daniel W. O'Neill, *Marrying for Life: A Handbook for Marriage Survival* (Bothell, Wash.: Messenger Publications, 1981).

4

Hanging From a Cliff

—Cherry

Beverly Hills, California—one of America's most coveted addresses. I grew up there, surrounded by all the material possessions a young woman could possibly want. The garages in my neighborhood were packed with exotic cars, and the refrigerators were packed with food.

But in my late teen years, in the middle of all that abundance, I came perilously close to starving to death.

How could it have happened? Did some sadistic person lock me away in a room without food for weeks on end? Did my body waste away because of a consuming cancer?

No. The problem was much more complicated, and to those around me who observed it, much more difficult to fathom. I was struggling with the eating disorder called anorexia nervosa, though for a long time neither I nor my family had any idea such a disorder even existed. Doctors had only then begun to discover what is essentially a sophisticated form of suicide—one that currently affects up to a million Americans.

Anorexia, dubbed by some "the dieter's disease," is characterized by a preoccupation with body weight, behaviors directed toward losing weight, and an intense fear of gaining weight. Anorexics typically refuse to eat, except for small portions, and often engage in excessive exercise routines to burn calories.

As the anorexic's weight loss exceeds 25 percent of her original body weight (the anorexic is usually female), she suffers from intolerance to cold and loss of hair. Anorexia can impair a number of basic body functions, causing cessation of the menstrual period, slowed pulse rate, and lowered blood pressure. If the anorexic abuses laxatives to force weight loss, as many do, she may also suffer from chronic constipation. Anorexia can lead to death by starvation.

Anorexia takes a severe emotional toll as well. Social withdrawal usually occurs as the anorexic becomes alienated from family and friends. The anorexic also battles with depression and thoughts of suicide—in fact, as we have mentioned, anorexia may itself be considered a slow form of suicide.

One unusual trait of the anorexic is that her perception of her own body is distorted. She sees herself as fat even though she may, in fact, be quite underweight. The protests of family and friends that she actually looks too thin make no impact on this prevailing "fat" image in her mind.

In my case, anorexia was tied to *bulimia*, another eating disorder that is also life-threatening. Bulimia is manifested by recurring, compulsive episodes of binge eating, followed by self-induced vomiting or abuse of laxatives. This disorder may be more difficult to detect because the bulimic's body weight may be within the normal range. But the behavior is no less dangerous than self-starvation; it can result in severe biochemical imbalance and even fatal heart damage, as in the case of Karen Carpenter.[1]

Both anorexia and bulimia are classified as impulse control disorders. Like alcoholism or drug addiction, they are complex conditions created by a number of interrelated factors. Noting the factors involved in my own case may help you understand how someone can become entrapped in such a destructive behavioral pattern.

A Little Perfectionist

I was born the first of four daughters in a family that was often under the watchful eye of cameras, critics, and

---

[1]For a summary of the physical and psychological effects of both anorexia and bulimia, see Vath, *Counseling Those With Eating Disorders* (Waco, Tex.: Word Books, 1986), pp. 39–56.

entertainment industry executives. My father, Pat Boone, was a popular entertainer who brought us on stage with him on a number of Boone family television specials. He sometimes introduced us as his four "misses"—emphasizing the pun because he had wanted a son.

In a family of high achievers, I grew especially eager to perform for the sake of the praise it won me. I was a little perfectionist: Though I made straight A's in school, I could often be found, even in grade school, studying hard till 11:00 P.M. on weeknights so I could make *A pluses*. I was always in competition with myself, never wanting to admit that neither I nor anyone else could be perfect.

Perfectionism is one mental mindset that can trap people into compulsive behaviors. It feeds the attitude that life *must* be a certain way, driving the person to strive relentlessly to achieve what is usually an impossible standard. For the workaholic, the goal may be achieving a certain high level of income; for me, the goal eventually became achieving a certain standard of physical appearance.

I heard of one bulimic woman whose recurring nightmare graphically symbolizes the plight of the perfectionist. In the dream, she walked a narrow high beam in a large cathedral-like building. (The building might well have reflected her rearing in a very legalistic church, which contributed to her problem.) The beam was two hundred feet in the air, towering above a floor covered with snakes and alligators.

The woman had to walk the whole length of the building on the narrow beam, and she knew the slightest slip would plunge her to a terrible death. Paralyzed with fear, she could not move forward or backward. She thought of jumping just to end the torment.[2]

Of course my parents were aware of the notoriously lax moral standards in Beverly Hills culture. They were attempting to instill Christian values in four young daughters surrounded by a neighborhood and schoolmates in conflict with those values. So they decided early on that in rearing us they would rather make a mistake in being too strict than too lenient.

---

[2]Vath, p. 82.

I wanted their praise, so I worked hard to observe the rules they established for us. The strict environment they provided me gave my perfectionist motivation a place to work overtime. But in my own mind, I could never quite measure up to my own expectations, much less theirs as I perceived them.

Instability

As I approached adolescence, two factors contributed to a sense of instability in my life. First, my dad's popularity as an entertainer skyrocketed. Top-of-the-chart records like "April Love" and box office hits like *State Fair* were a dream come true for him.

But once you've reached the top, there's nowhere else to go but down. As my dad's position in the entertainment industry eventually began to decline—a near-inevitable event in a world as fickle as Hollywood—our family life grew unstable.

My parents' marriage suffered some rocky times, and financial problems mounted as well. I found myself operating frequently as the family "mediator" when disputes arose. My dad's faith, which had always been a constant in my life, also seemed to be crumbling under the pressure. All this happened as I was heading into my adolescent years, which in our culture is a difficult and unstable season for most young people.

Children can respond to the uncertainty around them by looking inward and asking, "Is this my fault? Is there something I can do to keep these things from happening? If I were better, could I keep our family from the disaster that seems to be headed our way? Because my parents are going through a hard time, I'll make up for it by being really good!"

The second factor that introduced instability into my life during this time was the loss of three people who were very important to me: my grandfather, my great grandfather, and my best friend, who was only fourteen years old when she died. On the surface I seemed to handle these situations well. I thought I was being strong by maintaining my composure. But I realize now that I was actually denying the sorrow I felt and not allowing myself to grieve.

Looking back, I see how insecure my world was, and how desperately I wanted to hold it together. Control became an important issue to me, as it is with most anorexics and those suffering other compulsive disorders. Ignoring and suppressing my emotions was also a dangerous response to bereavement, which only intensified my internal pressures.

The Pains of Adolescence

In time, my parents reached the end of their "valley" and emerged with renewed marriage and faith commitments. My sisters and I also experienced a renewal. For me, however, spiritual renewal did not instantly release me from my deep uncertainty about life. In fact, the stresses of adolescence only intensified it.

As with most young girls, when I grew interested in boys, several internal pressures developed. I struggled for self-confidence and was critical of my physical appearance. I never gave up my virginity, but a couple of encounters with young men whose advances were unwelcome left me feeling guilty and fearful about sexuality. Any sexual involvement beyond the most innocent of kisses made me anxious. Meanwhile, my parents kept a watchful eye on my male friends.

Concern about my appearance was primarily focused on my weight. Though you could hardly call me overweight, I wanted to be more slender than I was. So by the time I was in eighth grade, I was using my mother's diet pills without her knowledge.

As my body grew tolerant of the drug, I had to double the dosage to achieve the desired affects of appetite loss and extra energy. In time, I was using so many pills that I felt compelled to practice an elaborate deception to secure my supply. I would call the pharmacy, pretending to be my mother, and ask for a refill of the prescription. Then I would pick up the pills and pay for them myself.

Finally the doctor called my mother to investigate the excessive pill consumption. I was discovered, but I denied it. My mom began hiding the bottle, but I would find it and stash enough to last awhile. When she realized at last that I would go to any lengths to get to her pills, she canceled the prescription altogether rather than risk my continued use.

I ballooned in weight, from 113 to 140. Considering my height and frame, that was still not an unhealthy amount, but it was enough to make me panic. In the world of Hollywood images, "thin" was best—and that meant rail thin. Worse yet, our family was appearing on television, and I worried about how I would look on stage.

Most aspects of my life at that time seemed to be out of my control and under someone else's. My social life was strictly controlled, and even my daily schedule was often dominated by the demands of our performing itinerary, which took us out of town to perform or make recordings for an average of one week every month. I can't say that it was a conscious decision, but I gradually seized control of at least one part of my life: my body.

As we noted in Chapter 3, impulse control disorders are a maladaptive response to something painful in the environment. In my case, the pressure to be and look perfect was more than I could bear. Added to that was the frustrating sense that everyone had control of my life but me. Real or imagined, that is how I interpreted events. My unhealthy response was to aggressively plunge into severe diet and exercise routines.

The "Plunge"

What I ate and how much energy I expended now took on new meaning—and intensity. The results were soon apparent as I dropped from 140 to 116 pounds. I received praise from everyone, including our family doctor, for losing the weight. That kind of reinforcement was a powerful incentive for me to continue, even when I no longer needed to reduce.

Once I reached a reasonable weight goal, I rationalized that perhaps I should lose a few more pounds to give myself some leeway. I was moving, in little steps, away from normality. This too is a characteristic of impulse control disorders. They do not happen overnight; they develop over time in small increments.

So I kept exercising and dieting, and the more I lost, the more I wanted to lose. I almost felt "high" at times over the exhilaration of being in control of my body, and the continuing compliments on my appearance by well-meaning friends only increased my sense of victory and fueled my zeal.

By the time I was sixteen, I had developed a strenuous, punishing regimen of diet and exercise. In the mornings I did stretching exercises and jogged four miles before school, skipping breakfast. Then I drove to a friend's house and rode a bicycle the rest of the way to school.

At school I skipped lunch, or had at most an apple or tossed salad. After classes I rode my bike again, took my dog on a walk, did two hours of calisthenics, swam a half mile and took a sauna. Convinced I had burned off enough calories to allow for the evening meal, I then ate normal portions for dinner.

Avoiding Detection

In time, people began noticing that I was getting too thin. They would tell me so, suggesting that I should eat a little more or exercise a little less. But I was so eager to maintain control of this area of my life, and so desperate to cling to the identity I was creating for myself, that I ignored them. In fact, I often dressed in several layers of clothes or withdrew to my room so I could avoid what seemed to me to be their attempts to control me.

My weight dropped to 92 pounds. I had become an expert at concealing my thinness, so my family didn't realize how severe the situation was. I spent more and more time alone in my room, isolated both from them and from my friends.

This kind of self-absorption is yet another trait of people with impulse control disorders. As the disordered behavior takes control of a person's life, all other concerns become secondary. Meanwhile, the person is too preoccupied to notice that relationships are atrophying and other important issues are being neglected.

One night I went into my parents' room as they were watching the news, and I fell asleep on their bed. My mother went to rub my back and happened to push my sweatshirt up a little. When she saw all my ribs showing through my skin, she was horrified. I looked like the victim of a concentration camp, little more than skin and bones.

When I woke up, she was crying and my dad was trying to console her. They told me I would see our family pediatrician the next day. When the doctor examined me, he said that if I didn't gain some weight, he would have to put me in a hospital where they would force me to comply. I had terrible visions of losing all control of my body and having my hard-won "victory" taken away from me.

I thought, *If I don't give an inch, they'll take a mile.* So I tried to begin eating a little more normally. But I hadn't eaten normally in so long, I had actually forgotten what was "normal."

In particular, I found that as I ate more, it was as if my body demanded more nutrition. So once I gave myself permission to eat, I soon found myself yielding to these demands by binging. I had begun to move from anorexia into bulimia.

Immediately after each binge I was gripped by a sense of guilt and a terrible fear that I would get "fat." To counteract the food intake, I made myself vomit and took large doses of laxatives. Before long I was trapped in a vicious cycle of binging and purging, consuming great quantities of food and then doing whatever was necessary to get rid of what I had eaten.

Not until this time did I finally realize that something was very wrong. Earlier, I had convinced myself that the anorexic behavior was "normal" because weight loss diets and exercise were such common behaviors in our society, and even more so in Beverly Hills. But I could not escape the reality that binging and purging was abnormal.

Still, I resorted to rationalization. I convinced myself that given the temptations of so much available food, vomiting was the only way to avoid the terrible consequences of huge caloric intake. This defensive measure of creating excuses is common to people with disorders when they begin to recognize that things are not as they should be. Psychiatrist Gerald G. May describes these reasonings this way:

> These rationalizations are not intentional lies; the person actually tries to convince herself that they are true. "I need a drink because I feel depressed." "I deserve a drink to celebrate." "I have to have these pills to help me sleep." "Life is too short, why not enjoy it?"[3]

However, the person knows at some level that these are no more than excuses, so the rationalizing actually increases distress and self-hatred. That growing interior conflict in turn intensifies the disordered behavior.

Resorting to Deception

It was a great irony: I wanted desperately to control my body, but in my efforts to control it I had totally *lost* control. I wanted to stop this behavior, but I didn't know how. The bulimia had control of me.

Worse yet, I was still afraid that others would take over my life totally—that I would lose my self-created identity—I refused to let anyone help me. In fact, if my parents or anyone else tried to raise the issue of my abnormal eating habits, I would vehemently deny that anything was wrong. Even though I was generally a truthful person, in this area of my life I developed a pattern of deceit to cover my behavior.

The deception took many forms. If I wanted to binge undetected, I shoplifted a box of cookies, a pack of Twinkies, a stack of candy bars. If I needed to purge, I stole laxatives from the pharmacy.

This kind of petty theft may sound like extreme behavior for someone who had grown up wanting to keep all the rules. But studies actually indicate that anywhere from 12 to 24 percent of anorexics and bulimics engage in

---

[3]Gerald G. May, *Addiction and Grace* (San Francisco: Harper and Row, 1988), p. 45.

shoplifting. They feel that it's easier to steal than to face the clerk at the cash register, who might question their purchases and uncover their secret eating behaviors.[4]

At home, the deception was constant. I would sometimes sneak into the kitchen after my parents were in bed to avoid detection. I would find a thousand excuses for getting away from the table, whether at home or in a restaurant, to purge myself of hated calories in the restroom. If I was caught throwing up, I blamed it on illness or the richness of the food.

I remember especially how at one point my father began dragging me to the scales every day to weigh me, insisting that I increase my weight to 110 pounds. I tried every trick I could conceive of to make him think I had reached his goal, such as guzzling water until my stomach ached before I stepped onto the scales.

One time when my mother was weighing me, I went so far as to slip some small dumbbells into my hip pockets. When she saw the scale read "111," she said, "That's wonderful, honey!"—and then patted me right where the dumbbell bulged in my pocket. The deceit was exposed, but I conceived other strategies.

When my parents realized that I wasn't getting any closer to their imposed goal of 110 pounds, my dad *raised* the goal to 115. His reasoning: "We offered you 110," he said, "as a compromise goal that was lower than we had actually wanted. But if you won't cooperate to achieve even a reasonable compromise, then we'll stop trying to compromise altogether."

The battle of wills was escalating.

I continued the fight by deception, growing more and more skilled with practice. But the struggle was exhausting. Living a lie can drain you of emotional energy. You are on guard every instant, looking for the opportunity to indulge in your secret behavior, plotting to escape notice, working hard to cover your tracks, fretting over whether you've left any evidence.

Oddly enough, I felt that my parents were forcing me

---

[4]R. Casper, E. Eckert, K.A. Halmi, S. Goldberg and J. Davis, "Bulimia: Its Incidence and Clinical Importance in Patients with Anorexia Nervosa," *Archives of General Psychiatry, 37,* 1980: pp. 1030ff.

to lie this way by trying to control me. All their attempts to help seemed like a conspiracy to coerce me into conforming to their image of what I should be—an image I knew they thought was designed with my ultimate health and happiness in mind. I felt trapped in the compulsive cycle of binging and purging, and yet felt guilty when confronted with circumstantial evidence by my parents. So an equally compulsive behavior developed: doing whatever was necessary behind their backs to accomplish my own goals.

Dr. Ray Vath, who years later became my psychotherapist, calls this growing complex of deceitful behaviors "the deception factor" in impulse control disorders. He notes that the dishonesty traps disordered people in more ways than one. For example, when they find it so easy to deceive others, they soon begin to continually fear that they themselves are being deceived. Even factual information offered by authoritative sources is met with immediate suspicion.[5]

Helpless and Hopeless

Not surprisingly, the battle was taking its toll on our family relationships. I knew I was hurting my parents by my lying, stealing, and other deceptive behaviors. I grew distant from them and from my sisters, and I felt threatened by their efforts to change me.

I also felt a nagging sense of guilt—not for my desire to be skinny, but for what I was doing to my family in my efforts to fulfill that desire. The endless succession of arguments and confrontations, marked by raised voices and tears, wore us all out. With each episode, the feelings of guilt accumulated until I succumbed to self-hatred.

When we went out to restaurants or dined with friends, I perceived any discussion of food to be directed at me. Any talk of weight I considered manipulative attempts to set me up for gaining dreaded pounds. I was suspicious of ingredients in meals cooked by anyone but myself—I was certain that a secret conspiracy was under-

---

[5]Vath, p. 146.

way to subvert my weight control objectives. I had become increasingly paranoid.

At times I made sincere attempts to change my behavior: eating without vomiting, foregoing an hour of exercise, having a substantial meal without allowing it to trigger a binge. One part of me genuinely wanted to be "normal." But in spite of my best efforts, another part of me somehow succeeded in undermining my good intentions. I felt as if I were in the grip of a huge emotional octopus whose tentacles had immobilized me.

In reality, I could not grasp the true dimensions of my disorder. At first I thought it was just a bad habit I could stop by a simple act of my will. But somehow I couldn't stop. So I felt helpless and hopeless, like a failure who had let everyone down—which is perhaps the worse feeling of all for a perfectionist who wants so badly to please people.

Though I didn't know it at the time, the roots of my disorder ran deep, entangled in the hurts and confusions of a lifetime. The problem could not have been caused by just one of the many contributing factors, yet all of them together led to disaster. As I see it now, the primary developments in my life that fed my disorder were the ones just highlighted: family instability and distress; pressures from the media and show business environment to conform physically; high expectations from my family and me; overprotection and control by my parents; and confused anxiety about sexuality. It was the formula for self-destruction.

Attempts to Find Help

When I first began the plunge into anorexia, I viewed the people around me trying to help as obstructions to my personal goals. *This is my business, this is my body,* I thought, *so back off and leave me alone. I'm not really sick.*

My attitude toward these people changed, however, when my behavior became so unmanageable that even I could see I had a serious problem. Once the bulimia developed, accompanied by undeniably inappropriate behaviors of shoplifting and self-induced vomiting, I realized that I really did need help. I believed that my family and others were genuinely trying to help me, and that they were motivated by concern for me. But I didn't always agree with the approach they were taking, and their strategies were ineffective—at times, even counterproductive.

I consented to occasional outside counseling when it was suggested by my parents or others. These sessions included several lengthy discussions, followed by even lengthier times of prayer, concluding with tears, a pledge of commitment, and an intense level of resolve to change. Each session felt like a spiritual and psychological breakthrough, but the effect soon faded.

I recall serious discussions with the pastor of our church, Jack Hayford, widely regarded for his insight, wisdom, and balance. He felt there was a buildup of tension inside me, an unrelieved stress that was manifesting itself in my inflexible approach to life. He believed I had two alternatives—life or death—and it was up to me to make the critical choice.

I told him and myself that I wanted to choose life. But my subsequent behavior fell pitifully short. Somehow I just couldn't make the changes that the choice required.

I was on an emotional roller coaster. After what seemed like a breakthrough in a counseling session, I would feel high. But when the habits reemerged, my mood would plunge desperately low once again.

Insights Were Not Enough

On occasion I gained an insight that would help me understand myself better. For example, a couple who were close friends of my parents once talked with me about my perfectionism and my striving to achieve. They speculated that perhaps I was living in my father's shadow and trying desperately to measure up to his image, to match his reputation for multifaceted accomplishments at an early age.

I assured them that my parents were applying no pressure on me to be such a high achiever. But they replied that even if the verbal message was absent, my perception of their desires could create the same pressures. Their observation made sense to me.

Another clear insight emerged when my parents came across a magazine article describing anorexia. They were encouraged to know that my condition had a name and was treatable, and I shared their excitement. At long last the unseen, unknown phantom I had been fighting had an identity, and I wasn't the only one battling it. But in spite of more medical tests and a session with a psychologist, we were unable to leverage that insight into developing an effective strategy for my recovery.

Somehow, I was mysteriously powerless—and increasingly overwhelmed. Each little inch I climbed toward wellness was followed by a fall—then waves of despair. Doctors, psychologists, pastors, friends, and family all tried to throw me a lifeline. But each time, no matter how firmly I grasped it for rescue, it slipped through my fingers, and I felt more despondent than ever.

I'll never forget the night I reached the bottom of the pit. I'd had yet another confrontation with my mother over my behavior, and I finally crumpled to the floor in a heap, crying out for God to take my life. I pounded my head with my fists, but I didn't have the courage to commit suicide. Since I wanted to stop hurting at all costs, I hoped that maybe God would answer this one prayer to put an end to my agony.

Later that night my mother came into my room to apologize for the confrontation. "I'm stuck," she confessed. "I don't know how to help you."

I told her I didn't know how to help myself, either, and I asked her not to tell my father, who was out of town. She refused. I feared the consequences if he found out, so I continued to beg her, growing near-hysterical.

She was adamant. "If this is your idea of my only way to help you," she said, "then I give up. I can't do it, Cherry! I give up."

Her words horrified me. "No, Mommy!" I cried. "You can't give up and leave me alone. Please don't give up on me!" I felt as if I were hanging from the edge of a cliff, about to fall.

New Husband, New Hope

Of course, my mother didn't give up on me, nor did the rest of my family. But they were totally baffled about how to help me. Nothing they did seemed to make a long-term difference in my behavior.

Not long after I turned twenty, however, a new ray of hope came into my life. I fell in love with a caring man who seemed sensitive to my struggle and supported me without being judgmental. Despite the disturbing episode during our engagement that Dan described in the first chapter, he and I were married, and I was thrilled at the prospect of starting a new life with him.

Sadly enough, hope was short-lived. On the honeymoon I bought a laxative to encourage my sluggish system to function properly. That simple purchase drew me back into another series of abusive, weight-reducing efforts, and by the time we returned home to our "new" life, I was back to all of my old tricks.

The deceptive techniques I had perfected with my parents I now used to conceal my worsening disorder from Dan. How Dan exposed my behavior, and the struggles that resulted when he did, graphically illustrate the issues that arise when you make the frightening discovery that someone you love has an impulse control disorder.

5

Denial, Discernment, Deceit, Disclosure

—Dan

Uncovering an impulse control disorder is not a single event, but rather a long series of discoveries, bewildering and disturbing. Typically, the process displays four aspects: denial, discernment, deceit, and disclosure. These are not stages, but rather strands of the experience that are intertwined in baffling and complex ways. Though more common problems like alcoholism or drug addiction may be easier to identify than lesser-known disorders like anorexia, their discovery involves similar scenarios of suspicion, spying, and confrontation that only gradually force the disordered person to admit there is a problem.

We disclosed in the last chapter how Cherry's parents came face-to-face with the shocking reality of her disorder one night when they saw her emaciated body. But it would be inaccurate to conclude that they discovered her disorder that night. The process of discovery had begun some time before, and the true gravity of the problem was not fully revealed until years later.

For many months, the family had been picking up disquieting clues that something was wrong. They puzzled over her abnormal eating habits, hours of frenzied exercise, increasing withdrawal, and mysterious physical ailments that defied clear diagnosis. Without a definitive cause to link these seemingly unrelated symptoms, they had no way of knowing how complex and dangerous her problem really was. Remember, this was prior to the days when anorexia became a hot media topic. It was much later before they even had a name for her struggle, and later still before they knew it required professional treatment.

My own discovery of Cherry's disorder came in a much more direct way: She confessed it to me quite early in our relationship. But her confession failed to ease the confusion and pain I increasingly shared with my in-laws. By the time we married, I was convinced that the problem was subsiding, only to find months later that Cherry's self-destructive behavior was in full swing—behind my back. Subsequently, I went through a deeper, more wrenching level of discovery that took me down a dizzying maze of disbelief and pain.

A brief account of that experience illustrates what we mean when we speak of the four threads of denial, discernment, deceit, and disclosure.

Denial

When someone first suggests to a person with an impulse control disorder that there might be a problem, the near-automatic reaction is to deny it. The alcoholic may protest, "I just have a few drinks after work, that's all." The compulsive gambler may ask, "What's the matter with having a little harmless fun?" The sex addict may insist: "I'm just looking for love; isn't everybody?"

The night Cherry's parents realized how thin she had become, they told her they would take her to a doctor the next day. Her reply was emphatic: "I'm not sick! I feel fine! I don't need to see a doctor."

Denial persists in spite of the concrete evidence— signs and symptoms readily observed by others in the person's life. Cherry, for example, could read the bathroom scales as well as her parents, but her judgment was warped by her own unrealistic definition of "normal." Alcoholics may have bottles tucked away all over the house; compulsive hoarders may not be able to close their closet doors on the bulging collection of junk they can't seem to live without. Lack of evidence is not the problem.

The real problem is that disordered people usually have some rather strong reasons—conscious or not—for denying their disorder, however obvious the disorder may appear to all those around them. Irrational though the reasons may be, these motivations have the power to distort perceptions of reality. Like all of us at times, disordered people tend to see what they *want* to see, and they most certainly do *not* want to see or admit to their problem.

What exactly causes the disordered person to deny the undeniable? We can identify at least four common sources of the problem:

1. The maladaptive motivation.

We must remember the insight provided by the adaptive model of behavior: People look for ways to cope with life, but some of the means they choose to cope are inadequate or even counterproductive. To the disordered person's reasoning, the disorder is an adaptive response.

The drug addict, for example, may be using cocaine as anesthesia to cover emotional pain from memories of abandonment, abuse, or betrayal. The anorexic may be refusing food because she seeks control over at least one area of her uncontrollable life. The compulsive overeater may be reducing immediate stress with each chocolate candy he consumes. The pornography addict may think he is bolstering his sexual self-confidence.

All this is to say that at some level, a disordered behavior performs some desirable function for the person who engages in it. No doubt the desired result of the behavior in question is more than offset by its destructive consequences. But this tends to escape the disordered person's realization. At least in the early stages, the disorder is an apparent solution, not a problem.

The disordered person may, therefore, view the concerned people on the border as the problem. In the early stages of her anorexia, Cherry saw her concerned parents as invaders of her privacy. In a similar way, the woman who feels compelled to hoard old newspapers, filling whole rooms with them, views her family as unreasonable when they suggest that she throw the papers away. Or the compulsive gambler who believes things would be fine if his wife would just stop nagging him about his choice of a recreational outlet.

2. Self-absorption.

A second reason disordered people may deny their problem is that the disorder makes them self-absorbed. The sex addict is so preoccupied with his next conquest that he fails to notice the emotional wreckage he has inflicted on previous partners. The anorexic is so focused on exercising and food avoidance that she fails to see that her friendships are withering.

As Cherry noted in the last chapter, in high school she developed an elaborate, exhausting exercise program that filled much of her day. She was so immersed in her daily routine that she resented any interruptions. Her entire existence revolved around her self-imposed four hours of exercise, and then, ironically, around gourmet cookbooks, menus, recipes, and caloric computations. Even phone calls from her closest friends seemed like unforgivable intrusions on her time.

Totally absorbed in her compulsion to lose weight, Cherry failed to notice that her friends had drifted away to form new relationships. Though the evidence of social strain should have alerted her to a growing problem, she was too preoccupied to respond or notice—or even care. To have suggested at the time that her compulsive exercise was killing her relationships would have produced vigorous denial.

3. Narrow views of spirituality.

In certain quarters of the church community, where much of our personal struggle and a significant amount of our counseling have taken place, we commonly find a third reason why people deny having a serious disorder: They have been taught that "real" or "serious" Christians don't have such struggles. Many church people tend to question the sincerity or spiritual commitment of anyone with an impulse control disorder.

This is an especially tough challenge for people raised

in homes where spiritual values and the expectation of living a morally exemplary life are taken seriously. If Christ actually dwells within me, they reason, then how could I possibly be an alcoholic?—or a sex addict?—or a compulsive gambler? And even if I acknowledge that these troublesome problems have emerged in part from hurts of the past, haven't I been "born again," made "a new creature in Christ"?

Compare spiritual rebirth to physical birth. We begin a new life at our conversion, just as we begin a new life when we first come into the world. Yet in the same way that our physical birth was only the beginning of a long and gradual process of growth, our spiritual rebirth is likewise only the beginning of a long pilgrimage. We don't run, walk, or even crawl spiritually from the very beginning; that only comes through a protracted process of trial and error, successes and failures—and an abundance of bumps and bruises.

In this light, we can see how erroneous it is to presume that Christians—regardless of how serious their commitment—should be mature and trouble-free. Imagine a parent attempting to make a baby walk before the child is physically ready, and then punishing the infant for failing to perform. The child might never venture a step after such an experience.

Too often we deny our humanity—our limitations and faults. This includes recognizing the limits of our own understanding. If our Christianity somehow hasn't seemed to help us with a particular struggle, if our faith hasn't provided us the total answer to every problem, we need not despair. Some elements of "the truth that sets us free" may well come to us from channels outside the church.

4. Fear of exposure.

Perhaps the most powerful motivation for denying a disorder can also be intensified by the expectations of others—we fear their reactions if we should admit to struggling with such a problem.

A few lines from a letter we received from a bulimic young woman caught shoplifting laxatives a few days earlier is typical of the disordered person's fear:

> I am terribly embarrassed and humiliated. I am a prominent member of the community and word has gotten out already. I just pray this doesn't end up in the newspaper.

Disclosure of an impulse control disorder can have frightening repercussions such as public embarrassment, rejection by relatives and friends, isolation from colleagues, and loss of social status or a job. Such negative consequences are highly motivating in covering problem behaviors and maintaining denial at all costs.

Forms of Denial

Denial can take many forms. Most obvious is an explicit verbal denial like the one Cherry made when her parents first registered their alarm. But reality is avoided in more subtle ways as well.

Often the denials are inner rationalizations: "This behavior isn't hurting anybody." "It isn't any worse than what other people do in secret."

Perhaps the most common rationalization says: "I could stop this behavior if I really wanted to." The person is convinced that the disordered behavior is actually under control. The classic and familiar example of this form of denial is the chain-smoker who insists, "I can quit anytime; I just don't want to right now."

Anorexics in particular fall into this trap because of control issues in their own lives. For those fighting fiercely to determine the shape of their bodies, exercise and self-deprivation feel like victories of self-control. At last, it seems, they are in charge of their own lives through regimented behavior—so of course they feel they could stop if they so desired.

When people in the border network continue to question a disordered person's perceptions of reality, denial may take the form of social withdrawal. Weary of conflict, the disordered person becomes angry, or simply avoids anyone who challenges his or her claim to be healthy and in control. The carefully constructed world of unreality is easier to maintain in isolation.

Yet another approach to denial arises from the disordered person's rising hostility toward those in the border network. We pointed out before that border people may be viewed as the "real" problem by those who are disordered. Not surprisingly, perceptions of other people's motives become distorted. Mistrust provides the grounds for further denial.

When Cherry was still living with her parents, she would occasionally gain weight as a strategy to neutralize increasing concerns about her health. But if her family or others complimented her on her appearance, she immediately assumed they were insincere—only flattering her in a manipulative ploy so she would gain more weight. If a girlfriend encouraged her to gain weight, it was only so she would look fat, Cherry convinced herself, and the friend would look better by comparison.

Later, after we married, Cherry's suspicions about the "conspiracy" against her intensified. When my mother prepared vegetables with butter added—the standard cooking procedure in the O'Neill household—Cherry was convinced she was packing in extra calories just to fatten up her daughter-in-law. Any help from people in the border network became suspect. Thus Cherry could continue to deny that she herself had a problem. It was others who had the problem, she concluded.

Denial on the Border

People with impulse control disorders are not alone in their denial. All too often those on the border also practice their own forms of denial.

Why would family and friends themselves refuse to accept the evidence of a disorder? Several of the reasons mentioned for the disordered person's denial are echoed here as well. A family member may stand to lose just as much as the disordered person if the problem is revealed: friends, status, income, even personal health.

A church leader, for example, may be reluctant to admit to himself that his wife is an alcoholic because he fears the judgment and rejection of church associates and authorities. He knows his status as a leader in the congregation would be seriously compromised. And if she happens to be on the church's paid staff, he may fear that she would lose her job.

A woman who suspects her husband is sexually addicted and acting promiscuously may avoid investigation of the matter. If her suspicions are true, she will question her self-worth and face the possibility of divorce and financial catastrophe. She may even discover that she has contracted from him a sexually transmitted disease.

Betrayal and Blame

In addition to the reasons for denial they might share with the disordered person, the border network experiences other pressures. One is that the discovery of a loved one's disorder is often interpreted as a form of personal betrayal. That was the case with me when I first began to uncover evidence that I was married to a bulimic. How could she possibly do something like that to me? I didn't want to believe that my new bride could be engaging in such disgusting behavior.

Just as disturbing is the possibility that a family member's disorder will reflect poorly on the family as a whole. Parents may be especially sensitive. They fear they will be blamed if their children are having serious problems.

In our culture, parents are often held responsible for the problems of even their adult children. Many psychoanalysts (as opposed to psychotherapists—more about that distinction later) attempt to treat a disorder by pointing the finger of accusation at the border network. It is not surprising, then, that families are reluctant to admit they have a problem, let alone seek professional intervention.

Whatever their motivations, the border network can find as many ways to deny the existence of a disorder as the disordered person. They may willfully ignore evidence as it appears: "I know those diet pills keep disappearing, but I must be misplacing them." They may put off investigating the situation: "Well, let's give it a little while longer; maybe we're just jumping to conclusions."

Or they may explicitly deny the symptoms: "You think she's losing too much weight? No—she looks just fine to me."

Often people on the border deny reality by making excuses for the inappropriate behavior. "I know she's sullen and stays in her room all the time, but she's just preoccupied with boys these days." "Yes, he seems to eat all day long, but he's under a lot of pressure in school right now."

Whatever their strategy, people on the border of disorder eventually find that reality will not be denied. The evidence mounts, the suspicions grow strong: They must admit at last that something is wrong, and it will not go away. Instead of denying it, they set out to expose it. But their motives are often mixed. On one level they truly want to help. On another, however, the border person's feelings of betrayal can influence a desire to retaliate and humiliate.

Discernment

The second strand in the tangled process of discovery might be called "discernment." Once a border person begins to pursue mounting evidence, a new dynamic emerges. They start to probe and question, investigate and even spy on the person with the disorder. In reaction, the disordered person typically grows defensive, elusive, and more hostile than ever.

My suspicions about Cherry's problem deepened when I realized that she was gradually losing weight, all the while denying it. For me, the red flag of warning was the gap between what she said and what I observed. There she was, a human stick figure wasting away before me as she insisted defiantly: "I'm not losing weight!" Surely, I reasoned, she could look in the mirror and see reality!

I had always seemed to possess a strong intuitive sense as to when people were lying to me or when something was wrong with them. I began to sense this happening with Cherry, but I wasn't sure how to handle it. She grew irritable, defensive, secretive, and before long my interior "barometer" was registering storm clouds.

One afternoon I happened to be driving by a large athletic field near where we lived. Cherry and I had agreed that she should not exercise so much—yet there she was, an impossibly thin-looking figure, doggedly jogging around a five-mile course. She happened to glance up and saw me in my car watching her, and at that moment she knew that *I* knew she wasn't being honest with me. This seemingly small discovery became another blow to trust and ignited suspicion.

Meanwhile, other empirical evidence began to surface. By coincidence I discovered that food was missing—at first single items, but in time, whole categories of food in our pantry would be gone, or perhaps replaced. I also noticed that Cherry was wearing layers of clothes, even in warm weather, to mask her thinness.

The husbands of anorexics and bulimics who have called me for help invariably report similar sinking feelings, which intensified as they made their own disquieting discoveries. One went to get a credit card from his wife's purse and was surprised to find a secret stash of diet pills. Another discovered stockpiles of laxatives hidden away. There are similar kinds of evidence for other disorders: the empty liquor bottle tossed in the automobile trunk, the drug paraphernalia stuffed under the bed, the dog-eared pornographic magazines tucked away in a drawer.

Becoming a Spy

Once the evidence of a problem becomes convincing, some people in the border network become determined to expose it, occasionally engaging in full-scale espionage. They look for clues and subsequently interrogate the disordered person. They may even set up situations to test the person's honesty—which, of course, feels like entrapment to the person who succumbs to temptation.

Today, Cherry laughs at what she calls the "CIA approach" I took—though at the time it was anything but funny. I went through the garbage looking for discarded food containers. I probed the pantry, taking inventory of the food. I marked the bottoms of canned goods and then checked later to see if they had been replaced.

For many border people, the role of spy extends even further to include rummaging through personal items like purses, filing cabinets, or diaries. They may trail the "suspect" in secret to find out what is happening away from home. They even question the person's friends, teachers, or coworkers to accumulate further damaging evidence.

Such espionage inevitably leads to confrontation. The border person produces overwhelming evidence and demands an explanation. The disordered person denies the obvious, makes excuses, and questions the motives of the "interrogator." Accusations fly and tempers flare, but the confrontation only worsens the situation. The border person feels driven to seek even more evidence, and the disordered person sees no alternative but to implement more sophisticated plans for a continued cover-up.

We should note that by this time the border person probably is not the only one discerning the problem. The disordered person may be growing fearful that something is indeed wrong, though such an admission would be unthinkable. The denial to others continues even as inner denial begins to erode.

Deceit

Ultimately, if the disordered person persists in denial, deceit must be practiced to shroud the problem. Even when the disorder is finally uncovered by a family member, the person may so fear the consequences of exposure that a disarming expression of repentance, followed by further deception, seems the only choice left. It doesn't matter that the struggler may hold to rigorous standards of honesty in every other regard. The disorder's desperate urge demands a different set of social rules.

Like denial, deceit takes many forms. Outright lying is only the most obvious strategy. Disordered people may weave elaborate and exhausting schemes to cover their tracks, concealing physical evidence of the behavior while secretly manipulating circumstances to provide themselves the occasion to drink, wager, engage in a sexual encounter, a drug fix, binge, or purge.

On occasion they will even resort to unlawful activity. Illegal drug deals are the classic example, but stealing is also a common strategy for hiding the evidence of various kinds of impulse control disorders. Cherry still marvels today that, despite her own high ethical and moral standards, she shoplifted laxatives and high calorie snacks. She feared that an outright purchase of those items in large amounts on a regular basis would raise suspicions among the grocery clerks.

Clues in the Garbage

I'll never forget the day I rummaged through our apartment complex garbage bin for signs that Cherry was binging and purging again. I arrived home from work early, and on a hunch, I peeked inside the large green dumpster. There I found a paper bag full of trash, with an empty brown sugar box on top.

I knew I had seen a similar box in one of our cabinets that same day. So I reached inside the bag to see what other condemning evidence lurked inside. There were candy wrappers, ice-cream cartons, empty cookie bags and doughnut boxes, a gutted chocolate cake tin, and an empty box of laxatives.

When I walked through the door, I greeted Cherry casually. Then I asked her what she had eaten that day.

"Well," she said, "I had melon and toast for breakfast and that blender drink for lunch—you know, the protein drink . . ."

"What about the brown sugar?" I queried, keeping my voice cool.

"What brown sugar?" she asked, feigning innocence.

"The brown sugar in the box in the kitchen cabinet—*that* brown sugar. How much of that did you eat? And what about the ice cream, candy bars, chocolate cake, and doughnuts?"

Cherry was baffled by my line of questioning. How could I possibly know what she had eaten? I could see fear in her eyes as she wondered whether I'd been spying on her all day. Yet she knew I hadn't; in fact, she had called me at the office in the middle of her binge to make sure I was busy at work and wouldn't appear at home unannounced.

"No, Dan!" she finally said. "I told you what I had. Why are you doing this to me?"

"You're lying to me!" I fumed.

"No I'm not!"

"Yes, you are—lying right to my face. And it doesn't even phase you!"

The scene was all downhill from there. I informed her of my discovery, yet she claimed it belonged to someone else. Then I began to fire away with other accusations: I had measured the levels of cereal, powdered sugar, and honey in their containers in our cabinets, and they had all gone down by two inches or more. Finally, I accused her of purging.

She was shocked that I would go to such lengths to gather evidence. But I responded icily: "How am I supposed to determine the truth about your food games when you're lying through your teeth?"

With that I flung my sunglasses into the wall, shattering them, and grabbed her by the arm. I pulled her into the bedroom, flung her on the bed, grabbed her purse and dumped its contents. I found laxatives.

She firmly maintained her innocence, which only infuriated me more. I finally shouted, "You want to act like a child, I'll treat you like a child!" Then I pulled her across my lap and spanked her. Moments later, I felt deep regret and confusion.

When it was all over, we were both in shock. How did a loving relationship deteriorate into such inappropriate behavior? Where would it all end? We were demoralized and overwhelmed.

Mutual Deceit

Notice in our situation a problem that is common when border people try to expose the disorder: The deceit of the disordered person's cover-up leads to the deceit of the border person's spying. That in turn leads to more cover-up.

The result? Each person tries to ensnare the other in a

cycle of dishonesty and mistrust. As with the disordered person, someone on the border may otherwise never dream of deceiving others. But the desperation of the situation seems to call for extreme measures. Disorder triggers disorder—inappropriate behavior emerges among the "healthy" border members.

One lie must be covered by another until deception becomes habitual. Dishonesty tarnishes the entire relationship, and those involved in the mutual trickery are left asking: Can I trust this person at all?

Disclosure

The fourth strand running through the process of discovery is disclosure: the disordered person's admission to people on the border that there is indeed a problem. It may come because of external forces. The person may be caught in the act, ending the charade. Or it may come because of internal pressures—the emotional exhaustion of leading a covert life may have simply grown unbearable.

Most likely, it will come in bits and pieces. The disordered person typically begins testing the waters, admitting to one drink, one pornographic video, one binge and one purge. If the response is supportive, more admissions may follow. If the confession provokes an angry reaction, the efforts to cover up may intensify.

Only two months after our wedding, as Cherry's hidden bulimic behavior worsened, we heard a sermon in church one Sunday morning about how love is totally honest. That afternoon, Cherry decided it was time to confess. We walked hand in hand to a nearby park, where she told me the details of how she had reverted to binging and purging, beginning on our honeymoon. She also admitted to deceiving me a number of times in order to hide her behavior.

Cherry was confident that I would be glad she had chosen honesty. She expected me to show the same kind of support I had given her when she first told me about her problem, while we were still dating. But her plan backfired.

I was stunned. To me, these were different circumstances altogether; now we were *married*. Were our wedding vows meaningless? Wasn't it bad enough that she had done those awful things without adding insult to injury by concealing and denying them?

I felt a cold steel barrier come up between us. I retreated into icy silence. No wonder, then, that in the days following, Cherry dared not risk disclosure again.

Is it any surprise that people with disorders try to conceal their problem from those closest to them? In a recent poll by the National Mental Health Association, only 14 percent of the people surveyed said they would risk going to a spouse, relative, or friend for help with problems like alcoholism, obesity, or depression.

Tangled Living

By now it should be clear why we refer to denial, discernment, deceit, and disclosure as *strands* rather than *stages*. There is no clear progression from one to the other. Instead, the four elements run throughout the disordered experience, tangled together in confusing, jumbled knots.

The people caught up in it all may waver between seemingly contradictory stances. The weakening anorexic may feel belligerent one morning toward "prying" family members, but guilty that afternoon as she shoplifts laxatives. The alcoholic's wife may angrily threaten to tell his boss why he missed work that day, but make excuses for him instead because she worries he could lose the job. Today the game may be concession; tomorrow, confrontation. Today, concealment; tomorrow, confession. The reaction of one party shapes the reaction of the other.

It's an exhausting, perplexing way to live. Shockwaves from the quake are rocking your life—and you are ready for things to change. As we said earlier, we can't offer you a fool-proof strategy for resolving the problem. But we can offer valuable insights from our own experience that may help you and the struggling person you love move from frustrating entanglement to a place where real change can begin.

Escaping from the Tangles

The person with an impulse control disorder hasn't much hope for healing until the problem is apparent to those in the border network who can create a therapeutic environment. Getting to that point may be less traumatic if people on the border consider these insights:

If you suspect a problem, don't panic. Fear of a disorder's consequences can pressure you toward paralyzing denial or untimely confrontation—two dangerous extremes. For even the most serious of problems, help is available. Maintaining hope is an indispensable mandate for the healing community.

The worst thing is to do nothing. Don't procrastinate when you have suspicions. Discover the truth. Waiting only allows the situation to deteriorate. If you pursue the matter and find you are mistaken, you'll be thankful— and relieved.

Give the disordered person a safe space to be honest. My reaction to Cherry's confession, described earlier, is a classic example of how *not* to handle that situation. Denial and deceit are less likely to persist when the struggler finds that a confession will not elicit condemnation and rejection.

You obviously should not condone the problem behavior. But in light of the emotional complexities involved in impulse control disorders, it is helpful to empathize with the struggler as an ally—not an adversary. Humility is critical here: Remember, no one is perfect, we are all disordered to some degree.

Cherry once had a registered nurse friend who would call her by phone to talk regularly. In the mornings Sandy always sounded sharp and alert. But whenever they spoke in the evenings, she seemed sluggish and fuzzy. We began to suspect some sort of drug abuse.

One day, over lunch, Sandy finally admitted to Cherry she was "borrowing" barbiturates from the hospital pharmacy to "relax" after hectic workshifts. If Cherry had reacted in self-righteous shock, Sandy may never have called again. But Cherry responded to her confession with supportive concern, and Sandy felt free to continue calling her and seeking her help. Whenever Cherry asked, "How are you doing in that area?" Sandy could answer her honestly, and they could talk about it. She had a safe space for disclosure.

Avoid entrapping the disordered person. You should certainly be alert for evidence, but don't set the person up for temptation just to justify your search. That kind of strategy is entrapment. It only draws you into the web of deceit.

Keep confrontations on target. The purpose of asking someone to face the evidence of a disorder is not to blame, threaten or punish. It only makes matters worse to say, "I'm going to divorce you if this keeps up. How could you do this to me? You're just like your father!"

The purpose of confrontation is rather to bring the person to a place where help can be sought. For this reason, the border people who lovingly confront a disordered person must focus on two subjects: carefully pointing out the destructive consequences of the person's behavior, and suggesting a plan for solving the problem.

Defuse potentially explosive encounters. If a conversation is likely to get hot, cool the atmosphere. Write out your thoughts in a journal, let them sit overnight, then reevaluate before you communicate them. Find a third, objective party you both trust to take part in the conversation. Choose a comfortable environment for the conversation and a time of day when you are more likely to be fresh rather than drained.

Keep conversations from getting derailed. Sometimes it's easy for the focus to digress from the issue at hand. This, however, is an evasive, counterproductive move, guaranteed to generate heat while the important subject is left in the dark.

For example, when a teenage daughter speaks sarcastically to her mother, the mother may get distracted: "Don't speak to me in that tone of voice, young lady. Haven't we taught you to respect adults?" Suddenly the dialogue isn't about the daughter's eating habits, which were the initial topic of discussion, but about the issue of respect—an important subject, but not relevant to the subject at hand.

Perhaps the most common dodge of the critical topic comes when one speaker questions the motives of the other: "You're just jealous, aren't you?" "You really don't love me anymore, do you?" "You don't trust anybody." "I guess what it boils down to is that you want me out of your life."

This happened frequently when Cherry and I would talk about her eating habits. I would venture a suspicion, then she would change the subject by saying I was suspicious by nature. So instead of talking about whether or not she had engaged in problem behavior, we would end up talking about whether I trusted her and loved her.

Resist such digressions. They only lead to dead ends, and more confusion and dissipated energy that could be applied to problem solving.

Share knowledge of the situation only with those who can become part of the healing community. One of the greatest pressures toward denial and deceit is the disordered person's fear of public exposure. For you, the corresponding temptation as you struggle with anger will be to punish the person by leaking information in ways that will cause embarrassment.

At the same time, you yourself may need supportive friends with a listening ear. But choose your confidants wisely.

Seek outside help. This is perhaps the most important strategy of all. You cannot carry the burden alone. Talk to a qualified expert or trained counselor. Find a support group like Al-Anon or its counterparts, which help the families of people with other disorders. Most importantly, when the disordered person is finally willing to seek help, assist in facilitating this decision immediately.

If you incorporate these insights consistently, you will likely find that the struggling person will call for help much sooner than she would have otherwise. Once that happens, the next issue is how to address the problem as quickly as possible. We must forge a "plan of attack"— but there are so many! And, tragically, most are doomed to failure.

6

The Quick Fix

—Cherry

When someone with an impulse control disorder finally admits to having a problem, people in the border network breathe a sigh of relief. *At last*, they conclude, *we can do something about getting this person fixed.* They feel a personal sense of responsibility to find and implement a solution. Having identified what they believe are the wrong and right behaviors, they look for an easy way to make the "right" behavior happen.

The difficulty, however, is that an easy solution or what I like to call the "quick fix"—almost never works with impulse control disorders. The border people who take such an approach tend in one of two directions, according to their temperament. Some hope to control the situation, trying by direct force to straighten the person out. Others attempt a more indirect approach, manipulating by expressions of their hurt and disappointment.

At best, these approaches may appear successful for a short time but, ultimately, fail. They may actually end up intensifying the problem. The real solution is something much more complicated, longer-term and more difficult—but far more satisfying.

When my parents first took me to the doctor to find out why I had lost so much weight, he was unable to isolate any physical causes for the problem. He suspected my eating habits were to blame, so he told me: "I have to believe you're the only one who can do anything about this problem. So you just have to stop losing weight and start gaining before you endanger your life. If you don't,

I'll be forced to check you into the hospital."

I was terrified at the prospect of gaining back pounds I had labored so hard to lose. But I had little choice. Because my parents had come to realize just how dangerous my condition was, they would make certain I followed the doctor's sobering directives.

On the way home from the medical exam, my mother stopped at the Beverly Hills Food Giant to pick up some of the most calorie-dense foods she could find: peanut butter, half-and-half, ice cream, cookies. After dinner, she presented me with a few cookies and a tall glass in which the remaining ingredients had been blended into a smooth, pound-promoting "milkshake." The concoction was an anorexic's nightmare—a "cocktail" crammed with calories.

When my mother left the room, I promptly went to the bathroom to flush half of the shake. I sipped the other half—and later that evening purged myself of even that. So began a new phase of my eating disorder: I moved from the food avoidance pattern of anorexia into the binging and purging cycle of bulimia.

Years later, when Dan discovered that such behavior had been continuing behind his back, he needed no doctor's orders to "fix" my problem. He devised a regimented eating plan for me that deliberately excluded any foods that might prompt a binge. Everything with sugar and almost everything with flour—except for an occasional slice of whole wheat toast—was eliminated from my diet. He was sure the problem could be licked if we just approached it with the right strategy.

Trusting Dan's radical new health plan, I threw myself into the regimen with zealous determination. But only a few months later I was hopelessly bogged down in my old habits, anesthetizing my frustrations with food, and then purging myself of its awful consequences.

My doctor, my parents, and my husband were all acting with the best of intentions to provide an immediate, concrete solution to my crisis. It seemed so simple: If you're not eating enough, eat more. If you're eating too much, eat less. Or as one psychiatrist (who should have known better) glibly chided a young anorexic we know:

"Just relax, honey, and try to eat like everyone else."

But it's not that simple. If it were, these disorders would not exist—or persist. The cure for an impulse control disorder was much more complicated than any of us at the time could have guessed.

Common Quick Fixes

What are the more common strategies border people offer a disordered person for a quick fix? Here's a partial menu.

Willpower. In this approach, people in the border network simply insist that the disordered person exert willpower to resist the destructive behavior. They preach self-control as the most obvious solution.

You drink too much? Just drive on past the bars. You overeat? Simply stay away from the refrigerator. You read pornography? Stay away from the magazine rack.

This approach can be summed up humorously with a comment we once heard someone's mother make: "You bite your nails? Well, then, keep your fingers out of your mouth!" Unfortunately, the humor is lost on the person whose habit is life-threatening.

Imposed regimens. Those in the border network who tend toward authoritarian attitudes, who somehow feel responsible for the disordered behavior, or who act in desperation may attempt to forcefully impose a regimen. Rather than expecting the disordered person to practice self-control, they assume control themselves.

Dan's binge-control regimen was precisely this approach. A wife's careful measuring of her obese husband's meal portions would be a similar solution. Yet another example would be the efforts of parents who attempt to schedule and monitor every moment of a teenage child's waking hours to prevent drug abuse. But in every case, the determined addict quickly develops techniques to circumvent the regimented routine because the underlying causes of the compulsion remain unaddressed and unresolved.

Threats. Border people who feel desperate, yet who don't think they're in a position to impose a regimen on the disordered person, may attempt to exert control through threats. "We'll put you in the hospital if you keep it up." "I'll divorce you if this doesn't stop." "I'll tell your boss if this happens again." "I'll spank you . . . take away the car . . . put you on restriction . . ." The behaviors then must become more covert. The disordered person naturally concludes, "If I'm not caught, I won't be punished."

Commercially produced quick cures. Sometimes border people put their trust in commercial products offering hope for a quick fix. The most notorious of these are the quick weight-loss diets and clinics that promise near-miraculous results in record time. Other products make claims for breaking nicotine and similar addictions. Some subliminal tapes for breaking destructive habits would fit this category as well.

Medication. Though medication may often be a necessary component of a successful comprehensive therapy, in itself it rarely provides a full solution to an impulse control disorder. We must also keep in mind that while some medicines (such as lithium carbonate or thyroid hormone) actually address one of the *causes* of a disorder by correcting a chemical imbalance in the body, others may only temporarily relieve or mask the *symptoms*—a less helpful approach.

Short-Term Results at Best

Why don't these quick fixes work? First, we should note that these simple cures frequently do seem to yield temporary results, providing welcome relief from the problem behavior—yet ultimately disappointing everyone involved. Clear examples are those victoriously slim folks in huge clothes featured on television commercials for weight-loss programs. They have obviously lost many "ugly pounds." But the great majority of dieters, including those who go to weight-loss clinics, eventually gain back all their weight—and often more.

Coercive strategies such as forced hospitalization, when not accompanied by therapy to get at the deeper issues involved, may work temporarily through imposed dictates. The alcoholic, unwillingly isolated from the bottle, has no choice but to get sober. The anorexic, strapped to a bed with force-feeding tubes in her arms, necessarily gains weight.

"Good behavior" may even be elicited from such a hospital patient if release is contingent on it. But in these cases, the disordered person is often involved in a cat-and-mouse strategy. "I'll do what you say to get out of here," they think, "and then I'll go back to what I want to do."

In my case, the quick fixes usually created immediate, encouraging results. The threat of hospitalization pressured me into gaining a few pounds. For several months after Dan imposed his Spartan regimen, I refrained from binging and purging and actually gained some weight. On the occasions when a counselor talked with me, I felt temporary relief—at times even elation. The session would end with tears, a renewed commitment to do better, and intense levels of resolve, which felt like an authentic breakthrough.

But, sadly, all these cures proved short-term. When the problem behavior returned, it was more deeply entrenched than before, bringing with it an ever-intensifying despondency and self-hatred.

A second point we must make clear is that in rare cases one of the above strategies may actually work. But these situations typically involve people whose disorders have recently emerged and are not yet habitual to any great degree. The "claws" have not yet sunk in very deeply.

For example, a person without a life-long pattern of obesity, who only began overeating during a limited period of high stress, may find that a commercial weight-loss program achieves enduring results. Or a teenager who has smoked only a cigarette or two a day for a short time may find sufficient "willpower" to kick the habit. For this reason we urge border people who suspect a problem not to procrastinate in seeking help. The earlier a disorder is diagnosed, the better the prognosis for recovery.

If a disordered behavior does respond to a quick fix strategy, it will likely manifest itself in a different form. When the root causes of the problem remain unresolved, the person selects—sometimes unconsciously—a different maladaptive response. Compulsive smoking, for example, may be replaced by compulsive eating.

This brings us to a third important point. We're not saying here by any means that some of the strategies we describe as quick fixes can't *contribute* to a cure. Certainly we recommend medication when a doctor deems it necessary. We also believe that willpower and a freely chosen regimen can make a difference in overcoming an impulse control disorder.

We don't condemn these strategies. But we are saying that none of them *alone* is usually sufficient to break the bondage of a deeply rooted disorder. It's a mistake to view any of these approaches, however good some of them may be in themselves, as a quick fix, an immediate and simple remedy. They all have built-in components that militate against long-term success.

Why Quick Fixes Fail

Why don't quick fixes work? A few basic flaws undermine their effectiveness in treating impulse control disorders.

First, quick fixes often draw false comparisons between a border person's experience and the disordered person's experience, when the two are radically different.

Superimposing our own experience on a disordered person is unfair. As in so many other ways, people differ in their limits and vulnerabilities. Just as one person's junk is another's treasure, so one person's aversion is another's temptation.

The man addicted to pornography may have no problem controlling his eating habits or refusing drugs and alcohol. The woman struggling with obesity may feel no desire to engage in promiscuous sex or gambling.

In fact, the very same root cause may produce within a single person a puzzling juxtaposition of self-control in one area and lack of control in another. For example, the shattered self-esteem of a homosexual teenager may drive him to disheartening obesity as well as admirable academic discipline—because binging on sweets and earning honors at school both temporarily soothe his inner pain.

An adult child of an alcoholic may never touch liquor, yet find herself addicted to prescription drugs to numb the ache of unmet needs.

No two sets of disordered circumstances, and thus no two avenues to healing, will be exactly alike. Most proponents of quick and easy cures overlook this reality of the human predicament.

Dan believed that the quick fixes he first pushed on me—willpower, disciplines, and behavioral regimens—would work for me because he had seen them work in other situations (though not in other situations involving me). For example, Dan had developed a mild habit of smoking in college, but once he had decided to quit, he gave up cigarettes in a single day. So he thought I should be able to exert the same willpower to overcome my problem quickly.

Of course, the similarity between Dan's nicotine habit and my bulimia were only superficial. My disorder had deep roots in the circumstances of my early years, a low self-esteem, a perfectionist streak, a stage image to maintain, and the cultural pressure to look as thin as possible. Dan, on the other hand, had taken up smoking over a period of only a couple of years when he decided to kick "cold turkey." He had never forged the bonds of a pack-a-day habit. His behavior stemmed more from a passing stage of peer association, and most of the surrounding culture actually exerted pressure *against* the habit rather than for it.

No wonder, then, that I grew to despise Dan's favorite exhortation to victory, learned long before from a high school coach: "Just toughen into it." Toughening up might be good advice for a distance runner, but it had little to do with the complexities of bulimia.

Second, quick fixes attempt to override the disordered person's will, thus setting up a futile battle for control.

We once received a letter from an anorexic/bulimic woman whose mother and father evidently were so desperate that they felt it necessary to take full responsibility for her decisions. The young woman wrote:

> I am a prisoner in my own home. I am twenty-two

years old and my parents dominate me completely. They say I am too sick to be left by myself. They are always checking up on me, even to the point of going through my purse and accompanying me to the bathroom. It is so humiliating! They want me to go to a doctor, but it must be the one that *they* choose. Even though I am an adult, I am made to feel like a child.

I could easily sympathize with this woman's feelings because I had endured some of the same strategies taken by those who loved me and were anxious to keep me alive. They were most certainly well-meaning, but they were misguided in their efforts.

The parents' desperation in this case was understandable, and to a certain extent (as I suggested in my letter of reply) the woman was permitting and even perpetuating their domineering behavior. Even so, their quick fix wasn't working. She was determined to lose weight and, ultimately, she would find a way around them.

In the beginning my family attempted to be directive and even coercive in their efforts to see me recover. My father, for example, demanded that I weigh-in every day and reach a minimum weight of 110 pounds, which to me seemed rather arbitrarily established. Punishments for my disordered behavior ranged from suspended privileges to spankings, which I received as late as eighteen years of age.

Nevertheless, I was fighting for control of at least one area of my life—my body. The battle lines were drawn. I binged, purged, and exercised in secret; I shoplifted food and laxatives; and I lied about it all. Not until years later, after therapy, did it become apparent to my border network that I was ultimately the only one who could choose health over sickness, life over death.

Third, quick fixes tend to deal with surface symptoms rather than root causes.

Most attempts at a quick, simple cure for impulse control disorders fail because they focus on external behaviors rather than internal pressures and pain. It is like dealing with a suicide attempt by simply putting Band-Aids on someone's slit wrists. If we don't ask the person, "Why do you want to die?" we will never address the real problem.

If a plan for recovery doesn't deal with the underlying issues of a disorder, improvement cannot be comprehensive, but will only be temporary. Superficial regimens cave in to the severity of deeply rooted self-hatred. Anxiety is fed by coercion. Threats only intensify depression. And medication is incapable of soothing seared self-esteem.

We may successfully put a lid on the psychological pressure cooker. However, if we don't find a way to turn down the heat, eventually the accumulating force of confined steam will blow it open again.

Fourth, quick fixes may fail to take into consideration the psychological inertia of habit.

Understanding the depth and complexity of an impulse control disorder helps us see why *simple* cures don't work. But appreciating the sheer force of habit operating in many disorders helps us see why fast cures don't work. Patterns of thinking, feeling, and behaving forged and reinforced over years, even a lifetime, will not be extinguished in a day or even a month. Most impulse control disorders take one to three years to overcome even with the best of therapy.

Habit has its benefits. We don't have to relearn life's basics every day. Once the ruts of habit are carved into our psychological terrain, we can follow the tracks without giving much thought to the process. Without habit, think of how much more difficult would be such simple daily tasks as brushing our teeth, making a bed, driving a car—even reading, writing, and speaking.

Like all good things, however, the power of habit can be abused. And when the psychological ruts run the wrong way, the ride won't be smooth until they've been worn down by repeated motion in the right direction. We may tell an alcoholic simply to put down the glass or an overeater simply to shut the refrigerator door. But those seemingly easy actions meet stubborn resistance in the disordered person's mind, which has carried tons of mental "freight" from years of repeated behavior and reinforced attitudes.

We like to compare the treatment of an entrenched

disorder to changing the course of a huge ship. The captain of a cruise liner once told us that at full speed it could take five *miles* or more to make a 180-degree turn. Or consider how tough it would be to stop an eighteen-wheel truck going eighty miles an hour. You can slam on the brakes as hard as you like, but you'll skid a long way before you stop—and even then you might still have a collision.

Quick fixes set up false expectations, and when those expectations are dashed, the disorder usually intensifies.

Perhaps the most pernicious consequence of fast cures is that they aggravate the problem when they fail. If the disordered person actually believes a quick fix will work, failure can reinforce the inner conditions that caused the problem in the first place—anger, depression, despair, fear, low self-esteem.

I felt an overwhelming sense of despair when my early attempts to conquer bulimia by teeth-gritting willpower all ended in dismal failure. I felt as if I were plummeting into a bottomless pit, with nothing and no one to help me—even myself. One night I crumpled to the floor, crying out, "I want to die! God, please end my life!" I pounded my head with my fists and wept until my face was swollen.

I didn't have the courage to commit suicide, and I knew it would be wrong. But the repeated failure to overcome my problem by the quick fix of willpower left me so devastated that I begged God to put me out of my misery.

Sometimes the disordered person knows from the start that the quick cure won't work. Then the person is likely to resent attempts of the border people all the more. Ironically, the very relationships most needed to build a healing community become a source of further tension, hostility and conflict. Thus quick fixes are worse than ineffective; they are actually *counterproductive*.

We once talked to a mother whose anorexic daughter was placed in the hospital against her will. During her stay she gained eleven pounds—immediate results that seemed to justify the action. But when the girl came home from the hospital, she was horrified to see herself in the mirror. Less than a month later she died from an overdose of barbiturates.

The immediate goal of weight gain was accomplished. Success seemed tantalizingly near. But the long-term goal of saving the young woman's life was not achieved. Her root problems were not addressed, but were, in fact, made worse by the battle for control—and so the daughter finally "won" the fight by making the ultimate choice to die.

What Will It Take?

Our observations about the futility and folly of quick fixes can be summed up in a single conclusion: Recovery from an impulse control disorder is a long, complex process. In an earlier chapter we outlined the three ingredients of a truly comprehensive and effective plan for recovery: medical, cognitive, and relational therapies. In this chapter we have attempted to show how there are no shortcuts to such an approach.

The good news, however, is that many small, simple steps may *contribute* to genuine healing even if none of them are *sufficient cures* in themselves. When people on the border look at a severe disorder and realize just how difficult the process of recovery may be, they might well be tempted to despair. But if we recognize that we have the power to do a great deal for those we love, we'll be encouraged to do what we can, while acknowledging that no single strategy will produce a quick or lasting cure.

Medication, though rarely enough, can nonetheless correct a chemical imbalance, providing a "level playing field" where the disordered person has a fair chance to win. Though it's not a panacea, it is one simple step that can be easily taken.

Perhaps the best "simple" steps come in those moments when someone in the border network profoundly touches the disordered person through a genuine, undeniable act of love. When I was still living at home, and the battle with my parents over my eating habits was at its worst, the turmoil understandably puzzled and eventually angered my sisters. I was alienating them so deeply that our communication was only minimal.

I remember the night I launched into a bitter, illogical

diatribe against my mother. While my volume was at its loudest, my sister Debby came quietly into the room, walked calmly toward me and placed her arms around me. Then firmly and lovingly she held me, gently patted my back and stroked my hair until the storm inside me had subsided.

Her acceptance of me at my worst—despite all I had done to alienate her—had a profoundly calming effect, which I found surprising and comforting. That touching, dramatic moment has remained vivid in my memory because I felt it was the first time someone had descended down into the "pit" where I was and just loved me right there in the depths of my pain and despair. She was not in a panic trying to pull me out, nor was she walking away in disgust and anger at my seeming refusal to climb out myself. She was simply there to share my burden.

Though full healing may not result from such a single pivotal event, it does grow out of a long series of such events. These small revelations, choices and victories, though seemingly insignificant in isolation, are nevertheless course-altering when taken together. Each one turns the disordered person one more degree toward wholeness.

In this light, we can see that the healthy alternative to the quick fix is, in the final analysis, a supportive attitude of patience and perseverance on the part of the border network. Healing humility will enable us to say, "I don't have a quick fix to solve this problem for you. I don't pretend to know everything it will take for you to be healed. But I'm willing to stick it out with you until you're free."

Above all, we must be willing to struggle alongside the struggler, sharing the burden, offering simple but persistent gestures of hope and help that will contribute to the healing process—a process that may remain hidden for a long time. Our efforts may seem insignificant, but they are like seeds planted, unseen beneath the soil until spring brings forth the first signs of new life to the surface.

7

Backlash

—Dan

When people in the border network rush in to help with a quick fix, they initially show considerable zeal and confidence about solving the problem. But as an old Japanese proverb says, "Frying pan that heats up quick, cools down quick." When the help doesn't bring immediate results, the zeal quickly cools and the confidence fades.

Instead of enthusiasm, we feel distress and disappointment, doubt and despair, fear and confusion. But perhaps the most pervasive feeling in the border network after quick fixes fail is a sense of *anger*. People on the border may feel hostility toward the disordered person—even toward themselves.

Such anger frequently leads to a backlash of negative behaviors: judging, punishing, entrapping, withdrawal, and more forceful attempts at control. These responses are understandable; often they are defense measures. In writing about people on the border of disorder, professional counselor Melody Beattie has observed:

> [Anger] helps us feel less vulnerable and more powerful. It's like a protective shield. If we're angry, we won't feel hurt or scared, or at least not noticeably so.[1]

Unfortunately, the backlash usually moves beyond defensive reactions. Unresolved anger can motivate us to

---

[1]Melodie Beattie, *Codependent No More* (New York: HarperCollins, 1987), p. 143.

vent hostility toward the disordered person in the forms of attack or punishment. Eventually the anger spills over into other relationships.

My anger toward Cherry eventually ricocheted off my mother just after we temporarily moved in with my parents. One evening Mom tried gently to protect Cherry from my criticism over her eating habits. To my own surprise, I exploded, saying something I'd never before even *thought* of saying to her: "Butt out, Mom!"

This unpleasant display of volatility is, in fact, only one of the reasons why we must engage the problem constructively. If we do not move from anger to forgiveness, we will only complicate the disorder, damage relationships in the border network, and undermine our attempts to become a healing community. The first step toward resolving anger is to recognize the ways in which we express it.

Anger Toward the Disordered Person

The backlash reaction can take a variety of forms, though we may not recognize them all as motivated by anger. In fact, so many of us have been taught that it's wrong to be angry, we may at first deny its reality in our lives.

The following statements typify the most common angry reactions we have encountered among people on the border when their first attempts to fix the problem fail. Though we may not make these statements explicitly, they represent the bottom line of our reactions. Every person on the border has reacted to quick-fix failures in at least some of these ways—many of us may have experienced them all. Perhaps you can identify with a few.

You're rejecting and hurting me with this behavior. You deserve to be punished.

Obviously, few of us would come right out and make this statement to a disordered person, and many of us would not even allow ourselves to think it in such blunt terms. But if we're honest with ourselves, most of us will recognize that disordered behavior can seem like a personal affront. We feel rejected, devalued, and betrayed.

We reason like this: If this person I love also loves me, she should be more concerned about my feelings, needs, and desires. Instead, she has used me, deceived me, manipulated me, and robbed me of my happiness, my health, my reputation, my material resources, my freedom, and my hopes for the future.

The punishment we inflict for this offense may be verbal abuse or even physical intimidation. When my carefully planned eating regimen failed to "fix" Cherry, I attacked her verbally—sometimes even with expletives previously alien to my vocabulary.

In fact, my attempts at control and the resulting failure touched off a powder keg of anger—anger and frustration that drove me closer to physical abuse than I would ever have imagined. As I mentioned in an earlier chapter, when I knew Cherry was lying to me about her laxative abuse, I boiled over. I shoved her, ripped her blouse, and ended up turning her over my knee and spanking her. My response was, of course, totally inappropriate, and only people who know me well could say just how angry I had to be to explode in such a manner.

The opposite of such outrage is icy silence and withdrawal, which can be as harsh a punishment as words and physical force. Sometimes when Cherry and I would argue over her eating habits, and after I had blasted her with accusations, I would retreat to another room and refuse to speak to her. In spite of her pleading, I would not say a word. To punish her I had put her in an "isolation chamber."

Sometimes punishment from the border network is more subtle. A wife may always be "too tired" to have sex with her pornography-addicted husband. A husband may chronically "forget" his household chores or "work late" at the office to punish his alcoholic wife.

Even a child may withdraw affection from a disordered parent or sibling to express anger. Cherry encountered this response from her sisters when she was still living at home, before the family was aware of the seriousness of her problem. The other girls thought her anorexic behavior was selfish and stupid, and that she was consuming the whole family's energies with her problem.

Feeling neglected, Cherry's sisters were angry that they had been put on their parents' "back burner" while Cherry received all the attention. So they began to withdraw from her and act coolly toward her.

Whatever the form of punishment our anger generates, the message is the same: You've done wrong, and you deserve the consequences.

If you had done what I told you to do, the problem would have been solved by now. So now I'll have to force you to do it.

This was my predominant response to Cherry when my quick fixes failed. I knew I didn't have all the answers for her problem, yet I thought I was putting forward some good strategies she should take advantage of. But they didn't work.

Of course, I thought she was just being stubborn. "No wonder you went on a binge!" I would insist. "You didn't follow the plan. I thought we agreed that you would stay away from peanut butter!"

It seemed to me that Cherry was rejecting my ideas. She didn't follow through with my suggestions, and it never occurred to me that she *couldn't* follow through with them. So the anger built inside me.

As a result, I redoubled my efforts to keep her regimented. If she wouldn't control herself, I would control her. I stepped up my surveillance activities and extended my management of the kitchen inventory. I even went so far one night as to conduct a strip search for hidden laxatives.

Needless to say, if the strategy of trying to control Cherry hadn't worked in the first place, it wasn't about to work this time just because I tried harder. The battle for control only intensified, creating a tense atmosphere of conflict.

That battle is repeated every day in families where some quick-fix regimen for an impulse control disorder has backfired. When imposed plans fail to control a person's drinking, gambling, smoking, sexual activity, or other destructive behaviors, the angry reaction is rooted in frustration. It is futile to take charge of such problems by force.

Cherry and I often compare the control approach to the paramedic who employs C.P.R. to pound a cardiac arrest victim's heart into beating again. We rationalize our iron-fisted domination as necessary for the disordered person's survival. But there's one big difference here between what we do and what the ambulance crew does: Because fear, anxiety, and anger motivate us, our "pounding" is more punitive than therapeutic.

I used to think I was alone in venting my frustration in aggressive ways. To my amazement, however, I have found that very often health professionals—even in a hospital environment—become exasperated with noncompliant patients. Consider the case of "Hannah," who was hospitalized in Seattle, her weight a dangerous 79 pounds. She rejected food and any liquid except water. Her doctor ordered I.V. feeding only to find that, when nurses had left her room, she ripped the tubes from her arm. Hannah's repeated criticism of the medical personnel attending her produced resentment in them, then anger. As her condition worsened, nurses force-fed her and, with obvious satisfaction, immobilized her with arm and leg straps. TV privileges and reading material were removed. A cycle of retaliation and punishment replaced the therapeutic approach that had initially been established. The medical staff had become part of the problem. They lost their compassion for her—she lost her confidence in their ability to help. Even they can be driven to the ragged edge of hostility and impatience.

You cannot be trusted. I must assume you are deceiving me, and to prove it, I will trap you in your deceit.

The failure of a quick fix usually pressures the disordered person into further deceit, and people on the border into strategies of entrapment. No longer are we satisfied simply to expose the deception so it can be dealt with positively. Our strategy becomes punitive—we set the person up to fail and lie about it, so we can victoriously prove our point that he cannot be trusted.

I became skilled in this activity, developing highly effective interrogation techniques full of psychological and semantic traps. I was also quite creative in setting up scenarios where I knew I would "win" and Cherry would "lose." I once went so far as to plant a tiny hair on the edge of a lid on a peanut butter jar. I expected Cherry to eat some of the peanut butter while I was away from home but then deny it later. I knew I could catch her in the lie by proving that the hair on the lid had been moved. Sure enough, she fell into the trap, and I had the satisfaction of confronting her with yet one more failure in spite of her denial.

Often when I caught Cherry this way, I vented my frustration. "You liar!" I accused. "I suppose you're going to tell me this is the only time you've done it. You say you're sorry—but you're just sorry you got caught!" Clearly, my reaction on such occasions was retaliatory and anything but helpful. Yes, I had proved my point, but to what end? It is a hollow victory followed by regret.

My anger gradually gave way to a general attitude of cynicism. Even though Cherry was honest in matters that didn't involve her bulimic behavior, the disorder touched on so many aspects of her life that I concluded I could not trust her at all.

You don't really want to change. So I'll leave you to stew in your own juice.

This form of backlash is a reaction of calculated withdrawal rather than abandonment. In a later chapter we'll talk about the temptation to despair and give up altogether on the disordered person. But here we mean something different—a less desperate, yet more hostile, response.

When the quick fixes fail, we may retaliate by withdrawing our support from the disordered person. We have not given up all hope; we feel disgust rather than despair. So we have a desire to see the person suffer alone with the consequences of the disordered behavior to "teach a lesson." If she *enjoys* what she's doing so much, we reason, then we'll let her get her fill of it.

We must recognize, of course, that it may be necessary to withdraw from what some have called *enabling* behavior—that is, behavior that helps people *maintain* a disordered way of life by sheltering them from its consequences. But we are getting at something different here. Withdrawal backlash is motivated by the desire to punish rather than to practice "tough love" or reflect despair.

The removal of *legitimate support* as a hostile reaction to failure was clearly the situation with Jerry and Sharon. Jerry, a compulsive eater, weighed a dangerous 290 pounds and struggled to control his diet as his doctor suggested. Sharon had become disgusted with his repeated binging. She felt betrayed when she labored to cook special, low-calorie meals only to discover that he had indulged in covert, high-calorie snacking. "You must like being fat!" she finally exploded. "I am going to dump the low-cal cookbooks and I'll cook whatever I like. You're on your own now—cook your own meals or go hungry." Jerry's personal crisis was now compounded. Losing Sharon's trust and support only worsened his predicament.

All four of these reactions to the failed quick fix—punishment, harsh control, mistrust, and withdrawal—have in common a single thread. Because they are motivated primarily by anger, they have a hostile edge that makes them much more than defensive measures or renewed attempts to solve the problem. Through each reaction, we are trying at some level to *get back* at the disordered person—however immature that motivation may seem. Though expressed in different ways, the last three statements are only variations of the first: *You're rejecting and hurting me. You deserve to be punished.*

The bottom line of all these accusations and behaviors is an *adversarial relationship* with the disordered person. At the time when the struggler needs most to have us fighting alongside, we view him as an enemy. Entangled with the problem of the disorder itself is the problem of a fractured relationship. Meanwhile, the anger and its effects on network people only multiply. The debilitating impact of the disorder spreads from the victim to the border network as our responses become embittered, frustrated, and embattled.

Anger Toward Ourselves

The disordered person is the primary target of our backlash, but not the only target. We may also become angry with ourselves. The most common self-accusations can be summed up in statements directed inward:

I've failed to fix this problem, which is my responsibility. Something must be wrong with me.

Parents experience this self-directed anger most sharply because they feel responsible for their child's successes and failures in life. We encountered just such a reaction in one letter from a pastor's wife. After listing all her family's spiritual accomplishments—the founding of a large church, a local radio broadcast, fifteen missionaries in the field—she admitted that their one stubborn problem was their daughter's anorexia. Then she asked the question that was eating at her: "Could we be contributing to our daughter's problems? I would just die to think we are the cause of her pain!"

Introspection can be helpful, even necessary, in the healing process. And, indeed, we *have* possibly contributed in some way to the disorder. But if we simply direct our anger inward, making accusations about our own incompetence or culpability, we do little to solve the problem. We do have a responsibility, but it is not to fix the disordered person. Instead, our challenge is to love in a way that sets necessary boundaries, yet recognizes the person's freedom to choose (more about that in a later chapter).

Before I met Cherry, I had a good track record of helping people with their problems, and I always felt gratified when they felt they had received help and hope. The tougher the problem, the greater the challenge—and the better I felt when victory could be declared. Then I hit the brick wall of Cherry's bulimia. My own wife was in serious trouble, yet nothing I tried could "fix" her.

What was wrong with me? My pride was wounded, and I felt deeply disappointed that this "channel of power" was somehow powerless. I experienced a tremendous amount of inner stress and doubt.

*I haven't done enough to fix this problem. So I must
search frantically for the right solution.*

In this scenario, we are angry with ourselves because
we think we have left something undone that could help
the one we love. Our guilt and anxiety spur a panicky
search for the quick fix yet to be discovered. Of course,
the frustrating reality is that no such simple healing short-
cut exists.

Cherry and I have met a number of people on the border whose anger is channeled into their quest for a cure.
They hunt furiously for yet another self-help book, another doctor, another counselor, or another hospital that
will cure their spouse, child, or friend. But the more fad
approaches they examine, the more failures they encounter, and the more angry and anxious they become.

Anger is understandable in these difficult situations,
but left unmanaged, it is corrosive and potentially dangerous.

What is the answer?

8

Learning to Forgive

—Dan

Anger, often in combination with fear and anxiety, lies behind the backlash response, whatever form it may take. We have been wronged, and though we may not want to admit it, some part of us wants to retaliate or to punish. Such angry feelings are normal, but as we have seen, they only undermine the healing process. If we fail to forgive the object of our anger—whether it be the disordered person, others, or ourselves—we remain locked in a prison of bitterness and resentment.

How can we avoid this dead-end road? The first step may very well be to admit that we are indeed angry. If we believe, as many people do, that anger is wrong, we will want to deny the feeling.

Those raised in a strong religious environment often consider anger to be a sin.

The Scriptures, however, do not teach that anger in itself is wrong. It does say that anger can tempt us to wrongdoing if it is not handled appropriately. "If you are angry, do not let anger lead you into sin; do not let sunset find you still nursing it" (Ephesians 4:26, NEB). Though anger in itself is no sin, *holding on to anger is.*

The same text of Scripture continues: "Be generous to one another, tender-hearted, *forgiving one another.* . . ." (v. 32, emphasis added). Forgiveness is the only way to move beyond the destructive consequences of the backlash to a hope for healing.

But what exactly is forgiveness? A definition offered by psychiatrist Robert McAllister describes forgiveness as "a giving up of resentment . . . or desire to punish"[1] Forgiving is a giving up, a *letting go* of the offender, whom we have held tightly in our emotional grasp.

McAllister's definition has special relevance for moving beyond the backlash response because, as we have noted, beneath each hostile reaction to the disordered person there lies at some level a desire to punish. In forgiveness we give up this claimed "right" to punish the offender. That doesn't mean we excuse the behavior or try to forget it. We simply abandon our determined attempts to punish it.

Admittedly, that process is more easily defined than accomplished, especially when we feel someone has injured us deeply or habitually over a period of years. In addition, sometimes those we love the most—parents, children, spouses, close friends—are the hardest to forgive because their offenses have the power to wound us more deeply. Perhaps a few insights can help:

1. *We can acknowledge with humility that we are all imperfect creatures and need forgiveness.*

If we can bring ourselves to admit that, as we mentioned earlier, all of us are disordered to some degree, then we must relinquish any sense of superiority we may have claimed. All of us fall well short of the impossible standard of perfection. This posture of humility puts us beside, not above, those who struggle. Without a self-righteous attitude it is far more difficult to hang on to anger—and far easier to extend forgiveness to our co-strugglers.

2. *We can identify any ways in which we ourselves have contributed to the problem—including our own backlash reaction—and ask the disordered person to forgive us.*

Even if our contribution to the problem seems insignificant compared to the behavior of the disordered person, we should admit our own need for forgiveness in the

---

[1]Robert McAllister, Ph.D., M.D., "Forgiveness," *Directions in Psychiatry*, Volume 8, Lesson 25, p. 4.

situation. That act will clear some of the emotional "debris" around the issue and free the person to hope that things could be different. It will alleviate anger we may be harboring toward ourselves.

This is not to say we must take the blame for the disorder, wallow in a sense of guilt, or wonder what's wrong with us. That would only confuse the matter. Instead, by recognizing our role in the problem we can see that we can now have a role in its solution as well, an exciting possibility to those who previously felt powerless. We can identify positive changes to make in our own thoughts, attitudes and behaviors that will significantly enhance our position in the healing community. There is hope that we can move from being a part of the problem to actually becoming part of the answer. It is a process of empowerment.

3. We can attempt to view the disordered person from a new perspective.

Anger and a deeply subjective relationship with the struggler clouds our vision, leading us to misinterpret what she may think, feel, and do. When we let go of anger, we can begin to replace our distorted view of the disordered person with a more accurate one—a view that produces caring and compassion.

The perfectly objective observer sees the children we once were, the parents who reared us, the social dynamics which shape our views, the traumas and losses that have injured or bound us. Viewed in this light, we can forgive more easily because we appreciate more deeply the causal factors behind the person's predicament.

Our friend, Jack, tells how as a young adult he was struggling to forgive his father—a man whose harsh, cold aloofness had devastated his children's self-esteem. The task of forgiveness seemed impossible. Just a few days later, Jack's grandmother happened to mention a scene from half a century before that burned itself into his mind.

His grandmother recalled that during the Great Depression, when his father was only a boy of six or seven, he helped support their poor, large urban family. Grandpa was an abusive alcoholic who failed to show up at work often enough to support them. So in the winter the child would bundle up in his rags, collect scrap wood wherever he could find it, cut rubber bands from old inner tubes in the city dump, and make bundles of kindling wood to sell on street corners.

Grandma told proudly of how industrious her son had been. But Jack was horrified by the account. Suddenly he could picture his father as that frightened little boy, shivering in an old, torn jacket, pulling his battered red wagon full of wood scraps through the streets, wondering whether his family would survive the winter.

Our friend had long known that his father had been raised in poverty and that his grandfather had been an alcoholic. But with this new, shocking mental scene of his father as a terrified little boy came a new and liberating understanding of the man. No wonder his dad had been so tough, so hard, so insistent on discipline and hard work! That abused child still remained inside him, afraid of the world and uncertain about the future.

After that occasion, when our friend Jack looked at his father, he saw the frightened little eyes of that child peering from behind the stony exterior of a man whom life had cruelly hardened. Though it had been difficult to forgive the man, Jack found it easy to forgive the child inside him. He had begun to see his father from a new, liberating perspective.

The more we understand the development, depth, and complexity of the problem, and the more we recognize just how stiff a challenge our loved one is up against, the easier it should be to release the offense. New perspectives give us the empathy we need to let go of resentment.

4. We can count the cost of failing to forgive.

Forgiveness frees *us* as much as it frees the offender. The emotional prison we maintain through our bitterness actually has two cells: one for the offender and one for us. Though we may intend to punish the disordered person by our bitterness, we ourselves actually suffer from it much more. Refusal to forgive cripples us emotionally, damaging our ability to give of ourselves, to trust others, and to experience joy. Unforgiveness also hurts us physically, contributing to such problems as muscle tension, headaches, ulcers, and even arthritis.

People on the border of disorder know from hard experience that the same troubled person can commit the same offense against them "seventy times seven" times— and more. Living with a disordered person means living with repeated failures and countless broken promises. So forgiveness must be an attitude, a process—a way of life.

If we are just now learning to forgive, it may take a while simply to identify all the offenses we need to release. Talking it out with a trusted friend or counselor can help.

Expressing Forgiveness

These insights should make it easier to forgive the disordered person and ourselves. But we need to act on them in a concrete way. Though forgiveness is no doubt a matter of the heart, words and gestures are important as visible, audible, tangible expressions of reconciliation.

At the very least our choice to forgive and our request for forgiveness should be spoken. If we can talk about the matter directly with the other person involved without further damaging the relationship, that is ideal. But if an "I forgive you" would only increase hostility from the other person, we recommend declaring that forgiveness in the presence of a trusted friend.

We should note here that the disordered person may not be the only one we need to forgive or ask forgiveness from. Disorders typically involve such tangled social webs that it is highly likely other people in the border network will have offended us as well because of their own roles in the development of—or response to—the problem. Shelley is married to Rob, an alcoholic. In conjoint therapy she became aware of the abuse he suffered from his parents and her anger burned against them. The healing process involved not only forgiving her husband's behavior, but forgiving his parents as well. Because Rob had been fired from his position as an airline pilot for intoxication on the job, Shelley found herself needing to forgive Rob's supervisor, against whom she had harbored feelings of bitterness for more than a year. Her success in achieving a forgiving attitude successfully neutralized a highly charged atmosphere of hostility that had developed around their alcohol-troubled marriage.

Often we are actually angry at the indirect consequences of the offender's behavior in our own lives. We counseled one husband, for example, who was furious at his wife's uncle because he discovered that a long-ago act of incest was a root of her current problem with sexual promiscuity. His anger was kindled to a great extent because his own expectation of marital fidelity had been frustrated by someone he had never even met.

We also knew a woman whose husband struggled with obesity and who felt the happiness of her own home life had been sabotaged by his constant preoccupation with food. She fumed every time they ate with her mother-in-law, who was often heard to exhort her grandchildren to "clean your plates; think of the starving children in Africa!"

Whether resentment has built up because of direct or indirect offenses, the result is the same. It builds a prison for us and the offender. We simply cannot afford to grow bitter—the cost is too high for us all.

The Redemptive Side of Backlash

Certainly the backlash of those surrounding a disorder can damage the potential of the healing community. But we should also note that even the angry reaction to the failure of quick fixes can play a redemptive role in the recovery process. If we pay close attention to the raw feelings and rough behaviors exposed, we may find them bringing certain issues to a head by clarifying our motives and demonstrating our limitations.

One night, I recall, I observed Cherry scavenging cookies from the floor of a supermarket while we were grocery shopping. I criticized her over her embarrassing lack of self-control, and we railed at each other all the way home. The argument came to a climax when Cherry reached a point of hysteria. She ran into the kitchen and seized a butcher knife from the drawer.

"What are you going to do with that?" I challenged.

In that moment she realized that her self-hatred had come close to its frenzied but inevitable conclusion. Standing there with the knife in her hand, she finally saw the true nature of her struggle. The whole anorexic and bulimic struggle was about killing herself. My furious backlash over her repeated failure had pressed her to acknowledge a twisted motivation she couldn't admit before: Her disorder was actually a slow form of suicide.

My own sobering revelation didn't come in such a focused moment of fury. Nevertheless, it stemmed just as surely from my angry backlash to Cherry's behavior. My self-discovery emerged through a long series of failed attempts to solve the problem. I learned a great deal about my own limits.

Through the stubborn reality of Cherry's disorder, I found that I couldn't depend on some tried-and-true strategy to "fix" everybody who came to me with a problem. I discovered that even if I could muster all the faith in the world to "move a mountain," the one mountain I couldn't budge was the will of another human being.

The failure of our quick fixes, and my backlash to that failure, brought about two surprising consequences. Through the process, I was humbled to the point of receiving new, healing insights, and Cherry was forced to choose between life and death. Those two steps forward proved critical in our journey toward recovery.

9

Bargaining

—Cherry

The now-famous "stages of dying" identified some years ago by Elisabeth Kubler-Ross are, in fact, stages of grief. When facing the loss of something precious—whether loved ones, relationships, dreams for the future, or life itself—people tend to work through their pain in a predictable sequence of responses.[1]

Those who stand anywhere near the "epicenter" of an impulse control disorder will lose a great deal in the "quake" and must work through their own kinds of grief. Some of them actually face the possible death of a loved one. That would rate a ten on the Richter scale. Others mourn the loss of a relationship that once seemed so full of love, joy, and excitement. Almost all know the pain of watching as circumstances dash their most cherished hopes for the future—or even the mere desire for a normal life.

Not surprisingly, then, some of the reactions to loss that Kubler-Ross have identified show up in a discussion of life-controlling problems. As we have noted, the interactions of the disordered person and the border network are tangled and often circular, so the process is not so neatly sequential, or even predictable, as her series of stages. But the parallels are clear: Denial must be overcome, anger must be worked through, and *bargaining*— the response we must consider now—accomplishes little.

---

[1]Elisabeth Kubler-Ross, *On Death and Dying* (New York: Macmillan, 1969).

A Failed Attempt to Bargain

My weight was at 97 pounds and slipping. Our quick fixes had failed, and Dan and I were working through the resulting backlash. Then one day Dan hit upon an idea for a different approach. Realizing that his attempts to control me had been futile, he decided to strike a bargain with me instead.

It seemed a reasonable solution at the time. *I'll offer her something I know she really wants*, he thought, *on the condition that she gains weight. That way I'm not controlling her—she'll be making her own choice.*

The bargain Dan proposed was simple: If I would increase my weight from 97 to 105 within two weeks, then I could accompany him on a tour he was leading to the Holy Land.

I desperately wanted to go. But an eight-pound gain in only fourteen days seemed an insurmountable obstacle. Part of me wanted nothing more than to please my husband, to gain the weight, and to go with Dan on the ten-day tour. But another persistent part would not permit me to gain a single ounce.

I was caught in a struggle between my rational conscious mind and my irrational subconscious. They were playing a game of chess and had reached a stalemate. Meanwhile, I looked on helplessly, a powerless pawn.

I didn't gain the weight. I didn't go on the tour. And if I had known then what I know now, I would never have held hope that such a bargain could work.

The Problem With Contracts

Dan didn't realize it, but with his offer he had made a stab at *contract therapy*—the strategy of putting into black and white a specific bargaining agreement with someone whose behavior needs correction. This therapeutic approach has been around for a while and is actually quite common. A behavioral contract usually states explicitly the mutual obligations of the disordered person and the therapist; the provisions for benefits or privileges to be gained through specific performances; the specific consequences of failure to meet the terms of the contract; and bonuses for complying with its terms.[2]

In my discussions with victims of eating disorders who had been hospitalized, I found that often the staff negotiated with many of the young anorexic and bulimic girls and women undergoing treatment there. They made bargains like this: If you gain five pounds, we'll give you telephone privileges. If you gain another five, we'll let you have a television in your own room. If you gain still another five, you can choose your own menus.

In some cases, such contracts evidently work. But sadly enough, most of the cases I know about failed to demonstrate significant improvements through bargaining. I suspect the same is true in most serious cases of impulse control disorders.

Why doesn't bargaining work? Several factors come into play.

1. The terms of the bargain are often arbitrarily established.

We knew a husband who told his nicotine-addicted wife, "If you stop smoking for a month, you can buy a new dress." In her eyes, the terms of his contract were based primarily on his own preference or convenience. What have smoking and clothes to do with each other? she wondered. Why for a month rather than some other period of time? Why should my wardrobe be influenced by his irritation about smoke in the house?

If the woman's problem were obesity, the offer of a new dress might seem to have some reasonable connection to the behavior—she would, in fact, need to wear a new size. But as it stands, the condition of the contract bears no natural relationship to the consequence, so its effectiveness is undermined. The arbitrary nature of the bargain feels unfair to the person whose behavior is expected to change.

---

[2]Robert M. Goldenson, Ph.D., ed., *Longman Dictionary of Psychology and Psychiatry* (New York: Longman, 1984), p. 178.

2. The terms of the bargain are often unilaterally imposed.

People on the border who wish to bargain commonly make a critical mistake: They unilaterally conceive, implement, and enforce the agreement. Consequently, the battle over control remains. Even though the disordered person has a "choice," the elements of that choice have been severely limited by someone else. What looks to one party like an agreement appears to the other more like an ultimatum.

In effect, contracts are often paternalistic. They may seem to be offering the disordered person a choice. But they actually put the person in the position of a child who must "choose" between a punishment or a reward.

Dan's bargain was similar. I was not consulted before he announced it. He had not asked me whether a different weight goal might seem more reasonable to me, or whether another reward might be more meaningful. He simply said, "This is the way it is." This kind of dictated scenario is doomed to failure from the start.

3. The motives of those making the bargain with the disordered person are often manipulative.

In many areas of our lives our motivations are, at best, mixed. So I recognize that the attempt to make a contract with a disordered person will rarely stem from a purely selfless motive. Those whose lives have been devastated by a disordered person's behavior will obviously be hoping to gain some measure of relief, and understandably so. At times border people must set some boundaries simply for the sake of their own survival.

At the same time, however, the disordered person can sense when a contract is approached *primarily* as a way of making life easier for the border network. When the main goal is to manipulate the person into appropriate behavior rather than contribute to recovery, the bargain will fail.

4. The disordered person simply may not have the capacity to meet the terms of the bargain.

With this insight we move beyond the faulty terms or motives of a contract to a more foundational flaw. The question is glaring: If the disorder has proven too stubborn and complicated to be solved by physical regimens, disciplines, coercion, and an array of other approaches, why would we expect it to yield to a simple contract?

As our psychotherapist friend, Dr. Raymond Vath, says, "You can contract to do brain surgery if you want to. But if you don't have the skills for brain surgery, you won't be able to fulfill the contract." The whole problem with serious impulse control disorders is that people cannot by a simple act of their own will change their behavior.

For that reason, simply contracting to act a certain way will make little or no difference in a disordered person's capacity to accomplish real change. In the simpler kinds of cases where contracts have worked, the bondage of habit and the confusion of motives are not so profoundly ingrained. But in this situation, the focus and strength of will is overwhelmed by the complexity and momentum of the disorder. The will of the disordered person has been splintered, resulting in a conflict among desires and motivations. My feelings when Dan offered to let me accompany him on the tour were typical: Part of me wanted to go, while part of me wanted to cling to the thinness I had assumed as my identity.

Should we wonder, then, that the "carrot-and-stick" approach of a bargain is doomed to fail? One part of the disordered person may very well be anxious, even desperate, to eat the "carrot" of the contract's reward and avoid the "stick" of its punishment. But another, competing part of that same person—bound by years of habit and fueled by self-hatred, low self-esteem, depression, or other complicating pressures—usually takes control. What reward could possibly be written into a contract with enough motivating power to win in such a battle? Consider the fact that many seriously disordered people are defaulting on the most attractive contract imaginable—the reward of life for those who give up life-threatening behaviors. And death for those who don't. If these are the terms of the agreement that so many impulse control disordered people fail to meet, how can any other contract possibly succeed?

In some disorders, physiological components may also

exacerbate the situation. My ability to understand and carry out a contract, for example, would at times have been impaired by my loss of reasoning powers—one of the effects starvation has on the human brain. Alcoholics might well have the same problem.

Simply put, contracts only work when those who agree to them have the power to fulfill them in the first place.

5. The disordered person may not be acting in good faith.

We discussed earlier the pattern of deception that complicates an impulse control disorder. The impact of that pattern on the effectiveness of contracts should be obvious. Negotiation is futile if it's not carried out in good faith, and good faith is in short supply where serious disorders are concerned.

The border person may well approach a contract intending to keep the terms honestly. But the disordered person may have no such scruples in this regard, being willing to hide, lie, cheat, and steal to maintain the mere *appearance* of keeping the bargain.

Many of the hospitalized anorexic and bulimic young women I have encountered illustrate this truth. The doctors would contract with them for "good behavior," and they would agree in order to receive their promised privileges. But when the nurses went on a break, they would exercise until exhausted, and when they were alone in the shower, they would vomit up their meals. They really had no intention of keeping the contract; they just wanted the staff to leave them alone.

6. Bargains deal only with the measurable behaviors that are symptoms of the disorder rather than underlying causes.

This is perhaps the most fundamental reason why bargaining fails to overcome serious impulse control disorders. The contract is actually a behavior modification technique that seeks to change overt *actions*. But as we have seen, behaviors are only the surface manifestations of much deeper problems.

We write contracts in terms of achieving measurable results—gaining or losing weight, abstaining from drugs, alcohol, or cigarettes. And we set the conditions within definite time lines: two weeks, a month, three months. If we were actually attempting to contract on *causal* issues, it becomes increasingly apparent how inadequate contracts are in achieving the goal of recovery.

Can you imagine the following contractual terms?

- "You will agree to boost your self-esteem by 50 percent in six weeks."
- "You will erase your memory banks of years of dysfunctional family relationships in three months."
- "You will stabilize your own biochemistry in seven weeks."
- "You will reduce your depression by half in the next ten days."

If we fail to deal with the underlying motives, then a contract will only fuel a disordered person's deceitfulness. When the anorexics I knew were pressured by hospital nurses to strike bargains, their attitude was: "I can beat you at your own game. I'll put on a few pounds and get out of here. But then it's back to doing what *I* want to do." When they returned home, their own disordered agenda easily won out over the contract.

In essence, the contract approach to serious impulse control disorders—like the quick-fix approach—is reductionist. Through such bargaining we attempt to turn what is actually a long, complex, relational process of healing into a black-and-white commercial transaction. The resulting failed contract produces the same fruit as the failed quick fixes: disappointment, disillusionment, renewed anger and, in time, a downward spiral of despair.

Can Bargaining Ever Work?

Having expressed our concerns about the flaws of bargaining, we must nevertheless note that a contract may have limited usefulness in some situations. After all, the practical application of love does require at times that we approach problems with the goal of negotiation—working out a solution so that everyone involved benefits. In those situations the goal is to clarify where we are, where we want to go, and how to get there from here.

Seen in this light, bargaining in the form of a contract might be applied constructively in several situations:

- when the behavioral problem has not yet developed into a long-term, serious disorder.
- when the contract has a limited focus as simply one part of a more comprehensive strategy, including medical, cognitive, and relational therapies.
- when the contract is necessary for clarifying behavioral boundaries and consequences arising out of health, safety, and legal considerations for those in the border network. Under this category we would include cases like the alcoholic teen who is forbidden use of the car unless he is sober; the drug-abusing husband whose wife insists she will report to the police any illegal substances she finds in her home; or the anorexic child-care employee whose employer threatens to fire her if she engages in self-destructive behavior on the job.

A Helpful Contract

A true-life illustration of this last situation comes from a family we know well who employed a governess for their children. Soon after Laurie began working for the Thompson family, they discovered that the young woman was bulimic and deeply depressed. In addition to repeated attempts to take her own life, she often took syrup of Ipecac, a medication which, when abused by those with eating disorders to purge, can lead to disastrous biochemical imbalance and even sudden heart failure.

Such behavior was obviously unacceptable for a person who would be entrusted with the care of children. But the family wanted to help the woman, and in light of her suicidal tendencies they were concerned that simply firing her might push her "over the edge." They called us for ideas, and we suggested a carefully drafted contract which they reviewed with a qualified therapist friend for feedback before implementing. The contract read as follows:

> I, Laurie, agree to engage actively in an open and honest relationship with my employers, Mr. and Mrs. Thompson, with regard to both eating disorder behaviors and mood disorder problems.
>
> I agree to abstain from using syrup of Ipecac during the period of employment by the Thompsons. I understand that any use of Ipecac will jeopardize my health and the safety of the Thompson children, and therefore will result in the termination of my employment.
>
> If at any time I am feeling depressed to the point of despondency and thoughts of suicide, I will inform my employers. They agree to discuss my situation in a supportive manner.
>
> I agree to periodically meet with a qualified professional who is competent to treat eating disorders and depression. I will bring a brief report, signed by the therapist, to my employers following each meeting.
>
> I understand that my performance at work and the extent to which I have abided by this contract will be periodically evaluated. The Thompsons agree to assist me in appropriate ways to overcome my disorder.
>
> (signed and dated by the employee and employer.)

This contract obviously has its limits, yet it does take into consideration several points we have made. First, the contract was not imposed unilaterally, but rather hammered out through negotiation and mutual agreement.

Second, the terms of the contract are not arbitrary. Since both syrup of Ipecac abuse and a suicide attempt on the part of the employee could endanger the children, termination of employment is a reasonable and even necessary consequence of such behavior. This connection is made explicit, accompanied by a stated concern for the employee's health as well.

Third, the contract attempts to bring the employee into a wider therapeutic approach by insisting that professional counseling for her become part of the arrangement. There is no illusion here that the contract in itself can deal with the deeper, more serious issues of the woman's disorder.

Fourth, the contract tries to minimize the possibility of deception in at least one regard: Therapy sessions must be verified by a note from the therapist. The terms here also emphasize honesty on the part of the employee, but by its nature the agreement is nonetheless vulnerable to being undermined by subterfuge.

The requirement covering binging and purging was restricted to the hours of employment, and an evaluation process was established.

Sadly enough, this particular contract did not achieve the primary goal of helping the employee curb her self-destructive behaviors. Eventually she violated the agreement, so she had to be let go. Nevertheless, three secondary goals of the bargain were accomplished, making the contract at least partially successful.

First, the employing family was able to affirm explicitly that they were not rejecting the woman as a person, but rather were placing limits on her behavior as it affected their own well-being. Second, the woman was made more aware than ever of the impact of her disorder on herself and others. Third, she was better prepared emotionally for the loss of her job because she was aware of the consequences of breaking the contract. Consequently, she didn't plunge into despair and attempt suicide again when her employment was terminated.

Bringing in a Third Party

In general, we recommend that any attempt at contracts should involve not only the mutual agreement of the border person and the disordered person, but also the collaboration of a therapist, counselor, or doctor familiar with the situation. The professional's insights are sure to be helpful in shaping the terms of the agreement.

An objective third party can also defuse the volatile emotions that may accompany the creation and enforcement of the contract. This was the case for us when Dan insisted I could not go with him on the Holy Land tour. Any strenuous objections I might have made about his "unfairness" ended when we visited a nutritionist. After a physical exam, the doctor confirmed that a ten-day international trip would be too dangerous for someone in my precarious physical state. He was able to show me that the travel conditions of our agreement were reasonable rather than arbitrary.

Above all, we want to emphasize that no form of bargaining should be viewed as yet another road to a quick fix. Contracts are not cures. If we use them at all, we must remember that even at best they can only serve as mutually approved agreements playing a limited, practical role in the overall treatment of an impulse control disorder.

10

The 911 Approach

—Dan

No one can tally just how many people die every year from the direct and indirect consequences of impulse control disorders. Some statistics are obvious, like the number of known deaths by drug overdose or drunk driving accidents. Yet to these numbers we would have to add as well countless cases of slow suicide from the unhealthy consequences of smoking, overeating, drug addiction, alcohol abuse, and other self-destructive habits.

Nevertheless, we don't have to count these deaths to recognize that even seemingly mild disorders have the potential to become life-threatening. For that reason, when assistance strategies fail, people on the border often feel they have no choice but to take what might be called "the 911 approach." Like frantic people calling the emergency phone number for help, they conclude that the situation has become a dangerous crisis requiring drastic measures.

For some, the apparent last resort may be a step others take much earlier. One example is joining a self-help group. By now most people with loved ones in trouble are probably aware that organizations like Al-Anon (for families and friends of alcoholics) exist. Yet they often wait years before even visiting such a group, because to many it is an admission of failure (see chapter 14 for more on this subject).

For other people on the border, psychotherapy and medication may come only as desperate measures late in the process. That was the case for us. When we packed our bags for Seattle to seek Dr. Vath's care, I said to myself, "This is our last chance. We've exhausted all other options. If this doesn't work, we've reached the end." We realize now that we should have sought these therapies up front rather than as a last resort.

We note these two sources of help in this chapter only to point out that even though many people view them as "911 approaches," they should not, in fact, be considered last resorts. Serious physical damage or even death may result if such help is delayed. Because denial of the need is often part of the disordered behavior, the border network may have to initiate the process.

Looking for Professional Help

Often, the family of a disordered person hesitates to seek professional care because of the considerable financial expense. They may conclude that they simply can't afford it. While we recognize how tough a hurdle this can be, at the same time we must ask whether such a family can afford *not* to get help.

A disorder allowed to intensify may finally result in massive hospital bills far beyond what therapy would have cost—to say nothing of the cost in misery for the disordered person and the surrounding family and social networks. Delay could even cost a life. We have personally witnessed this tragic reality.

How can you find appropriate professional help? Some national groups offer referral services for specialists (see the resource section in the back of this book).

When interviewing potential therapists, be up front about your concerns. In the very first session, ask questions like these: What is your approach to therapy? What has been your experience in treating this particular disorder? What are the important issues for you?

If the therapist's answers aren't what you're looking for, find someone else.

Keep in mind that many disorders have a biological component, so you may also need a medical doctor to take part in the therapy in a multidisciplinary team approach.

This can be particularly important when dealing with complex disorders such as anorexia or bulimia. A therapist, M.D., and nutritionist may be required to comprehensively address the illness. Because psychiatrists are trained in medicine as well as psychiatry (other types of therapists typically are not), they're able to apply considerable expertise where biological and psychological needs overlap.

The Trauma of Hospitalization

Seeking assistance from self-help groups and professional therapists, as we have said, should not be viewed as an emergency measure. But a few other strategies may indeed have such serious consequences for both the disordered person and the border network that they might well be called last resorts, or near-last resorts. We want to discuss two of these: *hospitalization* and *family disengagement*.

The decision to place a loved one in the hospital, with or without the person's consent, takes a great emotional toll on the border network, to say nothing of the patient. Repercussions of such an action are perhaps greatest when the disordered person is admitted involuntarily, as is often the case with minors. But even the "voluntary" patient may only go reluctantly, after the border network has had to strain its relationships by confronting the struggler with some painful realities.

When disordered people become patients against their will, they view the facility as a prison and its staff as their jailers. The battle of wills escalates, with those family members who had them hospitalized standing firmly on the enemy side. Trust is shattered, and anger usually reaches new heights as the patient reacts to "imprisonment."

We have talked and corresponded with a number of anorexic and bulimic teenagers whose parents placed them in the hospital without their consent. Their stories illustrate the necessity of such treatment in many cases as well as the risks involved.

One young teen—we'll call her "Marilyn"—had dieted

down to a frightening 75 pounds, dropping more than 45 pounds in a single year. Her parents saw no alternative but to place her in a hospital where she could be force-fed intravenously to keep her from starving to death. Months later, as she was still confined there, Marilyn's mother wrote us in desperation:

> I hope and pray that by the time this letter reaches you our daughter is still alive. She seems to want to die, although she never says it in those words. In the past two days she has ripped the tubes out of her arms, which are now her only means of nutrition. We never dreamed things could become this bad in our worst nightmares.

The hospital staff finally had to strap Marilyn's arms to the bedrails in an attempt to save her life. But if she is like the patients we described in our chapter on bargaining, Marilyn will eventually find a way to carry out her own disordered agenda unless someone helps her get to the root causes of her problem.

In fact, the problem is often exacerbated as such unwilling patients develop an adversarial relationship with the hospital staff. The patient may be so hostile and adverse to treatment that, as we discussed earlier, those who are supposed to help may grow angry with the patient. Consequently, the treatment may develop a harsh and punitive aspect, with the staff taking some satisfaction in the patient's discomfort and being relieved when she finally leaves.

But the problem won't be over when the patient goes home. As we mentioned in chapter 6, another teen whose mother wrote us was also committed involuntarily to the hospital. She didn't rip out the IV like Marilyn did. In fact, she gained the eleven pounds her doctor wanted her to gain while she was confined to "earn" her release. But less than a month later, she died from an overdose of barbiturates. It was a short-term victory but a long-term loss.

Planned Interventions

One alternative to involuntary hospitalization is to have what has come to be called an *intervention*. In this

strategy, members of the border network plan a joint confrontation of the disordered person to accomplish two
goals. First, they attempt to help the person face up to the
reality of the problem by citing facts they have observed
about the situation. Second, they try to convince the person to seek outside help—preferably in some kind of hospital or other treatment center.

Ed Storti, an intervention specialist, describes the five
typical steps taken in the intervention process:

1. The Inquiry.

Someone in the border network reaches the critical
point of concluding that a planned intervention is necessary and calls for professional help.

2. The Pre-Preparation Meeting.

The interventionist holds a face-to-face meeting with
the "core" participants—those who are intimately involved with the disordered person and want to take action. This meeting is scheduled as quickly as the crisis
demands, the same day as the inquiry if necessary. If the
interventionist determines at this time that it's appropriate
to go forward, the procedures, costs, and risks of the process are discussed. Core participants provide more information about the disordered person, themselves, and
others who might be willing to take part in the intervention.

3. Group Preparation.

This meeting brings together all those participating in
the intervention so they can hammer out the details of a
strategy for the confrontation. They talk about arrangements at the treatment facility, how they will get the disordered person there, what kinds of "leverage" they will
use (such as the threat of marital separation or job termination) and the options they have if the person resists
the plan.

4. The Intervention.

In her book *The Compulsive Woman*[1], Sandra Simpson LeSourd provides a helpful example of an intervention confrontation. In this scenario, Paul—an alcoholic husband and father—wakes up after a hangover one morning to discover that a group of people has assembled in his living room: his wife, children, doctor, and boss. The doctor explains that they want to talk to Paul about his drinking problem and asks him to sit down.

One by one those who have gathered speak. What they say has been carefully planned and rehearsed ahead of time for maximum impact and to make sure the conversation isn't derailed by arguments, tangents, or uncontrolled displays of anger. Each family member points out to Paul a clear example of how his disordered behavior has impacted those he loves. His wife recalls her fear when he came home in a violent, drunken rage. The children recount his broken promises and embarrassing public behavior.

Next, Paul's employer observes that despite his talents, his drinking has lost them business accounts and cannot be tolerated. Finally, Paul's doctor lists for him the physical consequences of his alcoholism, beginning with the damage to his brain and moving on to his throat, heart, stomach, liver, blood pressure, and sexual performance. He predicts that Paul may not last another five years if he continues to drink so heavily.

Throughout much of the intervention, Paul reacts with eruptions of surprise and anger. He denies the problem and makes excuses for his actions. He promises to quit, as he has done many times before. But the intervention group continues firmly to reflect back to Paul the reality about his situation.

The doctor notes that his earlier promises to quit have all been in vain, and that he needs help to change. A room has been reserved for him, the doctor says, in a local treatment center. He can leave the next morning and undergo treatment there for twenty-eight days.

---

[1]Sandra Simpson LeSourd, *The Compulsive Woman* (Tarrytown N.Y.: Chosen Books/Revell, 1987).

Paul protests that he is needed at work, but his boss says he has already arranged for a substitute until Paul completes treatment. Paul insists he is being railroaded, and he would have to think it over. He will only go when he is ready.

At last his five-year-old daughter takes his hand and makes the one unplanned statement of the session: "Daddy, it's now or never." Paul breaks into tears. The next day he leaves for treatment.[2]

5. Follow-Up.

The interventionist usually accompanies the disordered person and participating members of the border network to the treatment facility. After the patient is admitted, the typical challenges of the treatment period are discussed to prepare those in the border network. In the days following, the interventionist stays in touch both with the patient and the others to monitor their progress.[3]

We must note that not all interventions are as successful as the one LeSourd describes. But all successful interventions have one characteristic in common: They all focus on the undeniable facts of the disorder and its destructive consequences rather than making accusations about motives. As Vernon Johnson describes the process in his helpful book on intervention:

> It is *objective, unequivocal, nonjudgmental and caring.* . . . It is not a punishment. It is not an opportunity for others to clobber [the disordered person] verbally. It is an attack upon the victim's wall of defenses, not upon the victim as a person.[4]

Unquestionably some interventions have been counterproductive. We know personally of at least one in which the entire family structure was fractured as a result, and the disordered person only grew worse. For that reason, interventions should only be attempted under the direction of a therapeutic pro-

---

[2]LeSourd, pp. 276–279.
[3]Ed Storti and Janet Keller, *Crisis Intervention: Acting Against Addiction* (New York: Crown Publishers, Inc., 1988), pp. 20–25.
[4]Vernon E. Johnson, *Intervention: How to Help Someone Who Doesn't Want Help* (Minneapolis: Johnson Institute Books, 1986), pp. 61–62.

fessional who has experience in the process. Even then, the border network must recognize that it's taking a risk—but emergency procedures are often risky ventures.

Cherry's Hospital Experience

Cherry was threatened with involuntary hospitalization when she was seventeen and still living with her parents. But it was years later, after we were married, that she finally entered a medical facility. No planned intervention was employed, though her entire family agreed with her doctor that she had to go. She went voluntarily in the technical sense that she signed a consent form—but only under protest.

At the time Cherry's weight had plunged to eighty pounds. I was out of answers and full of anxiety—she seemed beyond help. Nothing seemed to work, and I feared she would die.

I consulted our family doctor about the situation, and he suggested a battery of tests. If nothing conclusive emerged, he would recommend hospitalization. Cherry panicked at the thought of being confined to a hospital bed, thinking she would lose total control of her body there, but she agreed to the tests.

According to all the tests, there was no physical cause for what the doctor had been labeling "chronic viremia." But the damaging results of Cherry's bulimic behavior were severe: hormone and electrolyte imbalance, anemia and a starved body that was consuming itself for lack of nutrition. Her digestive system had suffered such repeated abuse that her intestines had collapsed. Her menstrual cycle had long since ceased. As a defense against starvation, her inessential biological systems had shut down to conserve energy and sustain life.

With such disturbing evidence about her condition, the verdict was clear and the sentence was passed: immediate hospitalization. For Cherry, it was a prison sentence. Two weeks of solitary confinement were ordered for intensive examination. The following day, she signed her rights away at the admissions desk of Century City Hospital.

Cherry was assigned three full-time nurses who rotated on eight-hour shifts for round-the-clock surveillance. They were required to report to the doctor anything they observed regarding her condition. Her privacy was almost nonexistent, yet in the few moments the nurses allowed her to be alone—when they took meal breaks, or when Cherry was in the bathroom—she still found a way to exercise and purge. After ten days she checked out of the hospital a few pounds heavier but not really any healthier. Real progress only came later when she entered psychotherapy.

An Intermediate Goal at Best

Clearly, even when a disordered person gives consent to enter a hospital or other treatment facility, the causes of the problem are not being addressed unless hospitalization is part of a more comprehensive therapy as we described in chapter 3. Many substance abuse treatment centers do, in fact, include a broader therapy as part of their approach, so facilities of that kind should not be viewed as a last resort for the willing patient.

On the other hand, the most we can expect from mere confinement and forced abstention from the behavior is to gain some more time for the patient to choose life. That may, of course, be a legitimate intermediate goal in itself when self-destruction is otherwise imminent. But if the choice for life is not made, we have only postponed the crisis a little while.

In light of the possibility that intervention and hospitalization strategies may backfire, worsening the situation, we recommend that they be used only as true 911 approaches—when all else has failed. Especially in the case of involuntary confinement, such an extreme measure should only be employed when the health and safety of the disordered person or others is being threatened or impaired.

Sometimes in order to save a life the decision about treatment cannot be left to someone with a severe disorder, which may have left the person irrational and near death. But these cases are rare. Our associate, Dr. Vath, has on two occasions had to elicit the support of the courts to insist on such treatment, taking advantage of the Involuntary Treatment Act of the State of Washington, where he practices. Obviously, however, it is much better to obtain the patient's consent.[5]

With minors, of course, involuntary hospitalization may occur more often. We must remember that children are unable to evaluate the seriousness of the consequences of their behavior because of their lack of life experience. So they must be granted less freedom to choose than adults, and we may need to use the power of the law and the courts to force confinement if all else fails. Children who are suicidal, violent, or seriously ill from self-destructive behaviors must often be hospitalized for their own protection.

Family Disengagement

A second serious measure that may be necessary when the disordered person fails to make meaningful progress might be called *disengagement*. Disengagement calls for the person to separate from certain people (especially family members), places, or activities in order to find healing. We consider the strategy a 911 approach because it often requires near-heroic commitment on the part of border people as well as the disordered person to pay the necessary price in relationships, finances, and even career plans.

Sometimes certain members of the border network fail to become part of the healing community required for the disordered person's survival. This is often the case with parents, who may refuse to take part in therapy sessions or to cooperate with the therapeutic team because they maintain a denial of the problem or they fear being blamed for it. If they or others on the border go beyond refusing cooperation to an active undermining of therapeutic pro-

---

[5]Vath, Raymond E. Vath, M.D. *Counseling Those With Eating Disorders* (Waco, Tex.: Word Publishing Company, 1986), p. 172.

gress, the disordered person may need to seek distance from them for a period of time.

In a sense, disengagement from our family of origin is a natural and normal process. The storms of the adolescent years represent to a large extent a young person's cutting of the emotional umbilical cord from parents. It is natural and necessary, but sometimes progressive adolescent detachment has been stifled or delayed by controlling, domineering parents, resulting in what has been called *enmeshment*. In that situation, a therapeutic disengagement from parents may have to take the place of the normal process.

In some cases the person needs to get away from family members not because they are uncooperative or opposed to treatment, but because the person needs space to sort out relational issues involving them. A kind of clinical distance may be required to achieve a perspective on how certain people on the border have been entangled in the problem. The process of examining issues of control, self-esteem, rejection, and anger over past hurts may only be confused when family members or others unwittingly continue to control, reject, or hurt the person in trouble, adding to the weight of burdens that must be unloaded.

We are not necessarily speaking here of a total withdrawal from family or a severance of the family relationships. In some extreme situations that kind of drastic step might indeed be taken. But in most cases of disengagement, the disordered person must simply minimize contact for a time with those who seem to be part of the problem. After a while, the person's attitudes and behaviors can be reevaluated to see whether they have modified enough to be reintroduced into the healing community.

The same is true for other, non-family members of the border network. Especially in cases where young people are being heavily influenced by negative peer pressure, disengagement from certain friends and associates may be necessary.

How long a separation is necessary? That must be determined by the willingness of people in the border network to learn new ways of relating. Many anorexics who have moved away from their parents, for example, have written us to share their frustrations in attempting to reenter family life. Melinda wrote us after experiencing solid success in overcoming anorexia and bulimia at a treatment center far from home.

"I've been doing so well. My weight is up. I'm not binging and I understand more about my problem than ever. But when I go home to my parents, panic starts to set in. The same food is in the refrigerator, my father asks me to weigh-in daily, and old arguments come to the surface. I begin to experience temptations I thought were gone forever. And I feel myself slipping. . . ."

Here is a clear case where family disengagement must extend for a longer period of time. Family dynamics must be modified before healthy reengagement can take place. Old sensory cues may trigger responses that draw the recovering struggler back into problem behaviors.

Geographic Moves

The most natural way to disengage when the problem relationships involve people living nearby is a geographic relocation. Physical distance will usually decrease contacts if only because of the cost and inconvenience of frequent trips or phone calls. At the same time, a change of location can contribute to the disordered person's sense of building a new life and a new identity. A healing space is created.

This is especially true when the current location adds other complicating stresses to the person's life. For some, life in an urban setting is impersonal, frenetic, and frightening. Fear of crime, noise, and the financial pressure of city living may call for a move to a more placid, rural environment.

On the other hand, a person living in the country or small town may experience a different set of stresses that require a move to a more urban or suburban setting. Life on a farm or in the mountains can be inconvenient and feel isolated, with sources of help seeming far away. Or the gossip mills of small-town life can cause the recovering person social discomfort.

If a move seems helpful, it may of course require a job change or perhaps even a career change for the disordered person, and perhaps for a spouse as well. But sometimes such vocational adjustments are also required for healing. In Cherry's case, for example, the pressure of being on stage in the entertainment world intensified her anxiety over her appearance.

The same could be true for a number of other occupations. An overeating addict may need to quit a job in a restaurant kitchen. An alcoholic would need to get out of the liquor business. We even know of a pornography addict who had to leave his job as a theater film projectionist because the explicit content of so many movies he had to show reinforced his addictive behavior.

All these factors—family relationships, environmental stresses, career pressures—contributed to our own decision to move from Los Angeles to Seattle. We had suspected a move might be necessary, and our suspicions were confirmed when at the end of Cherry's hospital stay, her doctor told me bluntly, "If you don't get her out of L.A. she may die."

Why did we need to move? First of all, Cherry had to withdraw from the world of show business. The last thing she needed was the fear that millions of eyes across the country were fixed on her figure, wondering why she looked so "fat."

Second, she needed some distance from her family. The Boones had always been tightly knit, and though such closeness certainly had its advantages, it could at times feel suffocating. For eight years Cherry's career had been closely tied to her image as "one of the Boone girls." Because her healing required, in part, that she learn to make her own decisions, exercise responsible control over her own life, and bond with me in our new marriage (difficult for her as a performing "Boone girl"), she had to cut the apron strings. To their great credit, Cherry's parents were most understanding and very cooperative.

Third, the Los Angeles area had become an unhappy environment for Cherry. The huge city felt to her like a noisy, crowded rat race, oppressive, polluted, and threatening. She needed a more healing environment with peace, quiet, and a slow pace.

We chose the Seattle area as our new home for several reasons. Most importantly, we wanted to begin therapy with Ray Vath, whose Seattle-based practice had been suggested by my uncle, Rev. Ed Scratch, a close friend of the Vaths. Ray is now widely regarded for his success in treating people with eating disorders. In addition, my parents were already living in the area and could provide us with a new, supportive border network. We moved in with them temporarily, and the setting of their home offered safe, encouraging space for Cherry's recovery: In place of a mansion on the tourist-ridden corner of Beverly Drive and Sunset Boulevard in Beverly Hills, we enjoyed a small house at the end of a country road overlooking beautiful Hammersley Inlet, a bay surrounded by rolling, forested hills.

My parents immediately became part of Cherry's healing community. Though they had never had any close acquaintance with the challenges of overcoming anorexia and bulimia, they had considerable experience in helping hurting people. Mom and Dad placed few demands on Cherry, and despite her sometimes bizarre food-related behaviors, they refrained from judging her. In addition, their simple, "down home" wisdom contributed insights that became an important part of Cherry's informal "cognitive" therapy.

Costs and Risks

Despite our positive experience with a geographic move, we still note with caution that relocation has its costs and risks. Border people contemplating a move should recognize these before they undertake such a radical measure.

The most obvious cost is, of course, financial. Moving is always an expensive proposition, and transportation, living expenses, medical bills, and disrupted job income can add up to a crisis in themselves. Of course the disordered person's health is worth the money spent. But the border people involved in the move must keep in mind the financial impact so they can plan—and thus avoid adding more anxiety to the disordered person's stresses.

Career ambitions may well be seriously affected. A border person may have to sacrifice a satisfying, well-paying job with opportunities for advancement in order to make the needed move. Meanwhile, the job waiting in the next town may not be nearly as desirable as the one it replaces. If that's the case, the affected border person may have to process another round of anger and forgiveness toward the disordered person. Priorities will be tested periodically.

Another less tangible cost is the loss of immediate support from friends and family members who *are* a part of the healing network, but are physically left behind in the move. Regularly scheduled phone calls, visits, and correspondence will help fill the void. But a new local network must be cultivated as soon as possible to avoid the undermining influences of loneliness and isolation.

We once received a letter from a man whose wife had struggled with bulimia for six years. They had recently moved from Dallas to Los Angeles, and according to the husband, "the move has only made matters worse." She had grown lonely and withdrawn, and her health had deteriorated rapidly. Pressures multiplied until, sadly, the marriage ended in divorce. They may have moved too far too soon. Their situation illustrates the relational risks of moving. The grief of losing close contact with trusted friends, family, and associates may only intensify a disorder if we fail to establish a new network.

Aside from the issue of whether friends will be available in a different location, we must remember that some places will provide no better environment for healing than where we are now. A disordered person under pressure from family relationships may feel that getting away from them is all that matters. But what we are moving *to* is just as important as what we are moving away *from*.

We still grieve when we remember how an acquaintance of ours died from anorexia after moving from Los Angeles to New York. No one can ever know all the factors that contributed to her failure to recover. But we are convinced that it was a mistake for her to disengage by moving from one large city to another. Our knowledge of her struggles at the time suggests that she would have greatly benefitted from a quiet retreat in a more peaceful setting.

Worth the Risk

Our decision to move to Seattle was certainly not an easy one. Cherry had to cancel contracts for performances with her family—after costumes, choreography, and vocal arrangements had already been created and paid for. I resigned from a promising job as a vice-president with a well-known organization. We both left behind close friends, and many people close to us pressured us to stay.

We were putting everything on the line. That was frightening, because for all we knew, the difficult disengagement and "last chance" therapy with Dr. Vath might not even work. But we had to try.

Once we made the decision, however, we committed ourselves totally without looking back. We knew that Cherry's well-being was more important than anything else. Our disengagement allowed us to focus on her survival as the primary project of our lives, taking priority over everything else. Once that priority was established, things began to change.

In retrospect, we know now that our disengagement from Los Angeles was the best move we have ever made. By making that difficult choice, we reconfirmed our commitment to each other in a concrete way, and we actually embarked on a new adventure together that transformed us forever. In the long run, we lost very little and gained much more. Family relationships, friendships, finances, and vocational goals have been restored and even strengthened beyond our expectations.

11

The Codependent—and Other Roles That Don't Work

—Cherry and Dan

The long process of recovery from impulse control disorders is like a drama, with people in the border network playing major roles. Some people take on a series of roles, trying out but discarding first one and then another, hoping to find one that works. Others juggle several roles at once as they interact with the disordered person and others in the "supporting cast." Some of the roles they assume contribute greatly to healing, but others make healing more difficult—or even feed the disordered behavior.

In this chapter we want to examine the unhealthy parts commonly played as people position themselves toward a disordered loved one. Then in the next chapter we will look at positive roles—ways of relating that enhance recovery. But first we want to describe one particularly complex and destructive role that, sadly enough, some people on the border play for a whole lifetime. It's the part played by the *codependent*.

What Exactly Is Codependency?

The term *codependent* has in recent years become commonplace in discussions of impulse control disorders. Mental health professionals, support groups, and even people generally unfamiliar with life-controlling problems toss the word around frequently, sometimes with a narrowly defined meaning, but more often as a vague catch-all term for anyone on the border of disorder. A brief look at the word's history will help us clarify how we intend to use it in our discussion.

Originally, the idea of codependency emerged in the 1970s in chemical dependency treatment centers to describe an unhealthy pattern of coping with life that develops as a reaction to another person's abuse of drugs or alcohol. Codependents were said to be people whose lives had become unmanageable as a result of living in a committed relationship with a substance abuser. In time, the definition evolved to include people affected by and involved in perpetuating the behaviors of loved ones who struggle with *any* kind of impulse control disorder—or other inappropriate behavior.

As author Melodie Beattie describes the new term's emergence in her book *Codependent No More,* the designated "codependent" population expanded quickly as the label grew to include more varieties of unhealthy relationships:

> As professionals began to understand codependency better, more groups of people appeared to have it: adult children of alcoholics, people in relationships with emotionally or mentally disturbed persons; people in relationships with chronically ill people; parents of children with behavior problems; people in relationships with irresponsible people; professionals— nurses, social workers and others in "helping" occupations. Even recovering alcoholics and addicts noticed they were codependent and perhaps had been long before becoming chemically dependent. Codependents started cropping up everywhere.[1]

Not surprisingly, the further the term was stretched, the less useful it became.

---

[1]Melodie Beattie, *Codependent No More* (San Francisco: A Hazelden Book/ HarperCollins, 1987), pp. 29–30. We are indebted to Beattie's discussion of how to define codependency in Chapter 3 of this book.

Disorder or Normal Reaction?

In time, a debate emerged: Is codependency itself a disorder, or is it simply a normal reaction to an abnormal person? Some views suggest that codependents have an ongoing problem themselves, independent of the disordered person in their lives. They seem to want and need troubled people around them in order to be "happy" in an unhealthy way.

Codependency, at least as it is most often described, does in fact seem to be much more than a misguided reaction to a particular disordered person. The more serious nature of the problem is evident in two ways. First, when codependents end their relationship with a troubled person, they often seek out another troubled person and repeat their codependent behaviors in the new relationship. These unhealthy patterns of coping thus prevail throughout the codependent's life unless a conscious effort is made to change.

Meg illustrates the codependent pattern clearly. She grew up with an alcoholic father. After six years of a stormy marriage, Meg divorced her husband when she discovered he had had a series of affairs and was abusing drugs. She was devastated, but a month later she was dating again.

Her new flame turned out to be an alcoholic. He promised to sober up if she would marry him, and she believed him. He never kept his promise. After a second divorce, she swore she would never marry again. But she dated a series of men, all chemically dependent, and ended up moving in with one.

After that relationship crumbled, Meg lamented: "I don't go looking for these bums. I just seem to attract them." Yet at some level she apparently felt most comfortable with men who had impulse control disorders.

Traits of the Codependent

There is a second characteristic of codependency which indicates that it is more than an unhealthy reaction in a specific, disordered situation. The thoughts, feelings,

and behaviors that have been most often labeled codependent extend far beyond one relationship to include all
of life in general. The typical codependent has been described as exhibiting these traits:

- *caretaking*—a compulsive desire to "take care of" others and to feel responsible for their thoughts, feelings, needs and behaviors.
- *low self-esteem*—feelings of shame, guilt, rejection,
  unworthiness, and victimization.
- *mistrust*—inability to trust themselves and others.
- *denial*—willingness to believe lies and to ignore serious problems or pretend they don't exist.
- *anger*—a perpetual burden of resentment and bitterness, leading to depression or outbursts of temper.
- *dependency*—the feeling of being trapped in relationships, with an expectation that only others can provide them with happiness.
- *repression*—pushing uncomfortable thoughts and
  feelings out of their awareness.
- *obsession*—an inability to keep from thinking, talking, and worrying about other people's behavior.
- *weak boundaries*—allowing others to hurt and take
  advantage of them.
- *control*—the belief that they know best how things
  should turn out and how people should behave,
  with corresponding efforts to coerce, dominate or
  passively manipulate others.

Codependents may often experience lethargy, suicidal
thoughts, hopelessness, sexual difficulties, inability to
concentrate, and their own impulse control disorders such
as overeating, alcoholism, and drug addiction.

These characteristics obviously encompass much more
than a single unhealthy relationship. Even when they
seem to have emerged in the context of a particular loved
one's disorder, they ultimately extend beyond that situation until they grow serious enough to constitute a disorder in themselves. Codependent patterns represent a
maladaptive response to life just as clearly as the impulse
control disorder that triggers them.

At some level, codependents hope to meet some need

of their own by acting this way toward troubled people. Perhaps they cultivate a sense of false security by controlling others. Their self-esteem may get a brief boost from the perception that another person desperately needs their intervention. They may hope to soothe a guilty conscience by surrounding themselves with people whose misbehavior makes their own seem harmless by comparison.

Whatever their motivation, codependent strategies don't work. In the words of counselor Scott Egleston, "Codependency is a way of getting needs met that doesn't get needs met."[2]

A Working Definition

In this light, we need to distinguish as far as possible between more-or-less "normal" (though ineffective) ways of coping with a disordered person and a long-term tendency to seek out and settle down on the border of disorder. Consequently, we offer this working definition: *Codependency is a pattern of involvement with disordered people in which the disorder fulfills some maladaptive purpose for the person who, consciously or unconsciously, feels drawn to such relationships.*

Given that definition, it should be clear that the focus of this book is not on codependency. Unquestionably, denial, deceit, control, anger, and bargaining are strategies in the maladaptive repertoire of the codependent. Yet these are also understandable—though counterproductive—reactions to particular disorders on the part of those who feel no compulsion to be involved with troubled people. Many whose lives and relationships are otherwise healthy simply find themselves quite unwillingly on the border of disorder without the appropriate tools and skills to cope. Our experience can provide these people some insights for becoming part of the disordered person's healing community: the therapeutic border network.

This is not to say, of course, that people who struggle with a codependent pattern can't benefit from what we

[2]Beattie, p. 36.

have said. They need even more urgently to learn about the pitfalls of denial, quick fixes, backlashing, and bargaining. But people on the border who recognize themselves in the list of codependent traits on page 152 should consider seeking help for themselves as well as for the disordered person they love.

Test Yourself for Codependency

The following test for people who think they may be codependent is taken from Sandra LeSourd Simpson's book *The Compulsive Woman*. If you check more than a few of these statements as accurate descriptions of yourself and your relationship to a disordered person, we recommend you consider finding help (see further resources at the back of the book).

_____ My good feelings about who I am stem from being liked by you.

_____ My good feelings about who I am stem from receiving approval from you.

_____ Your struggles affect my serenity. My mental attention focuses on solving or relieving your pain.

_____ My mental attention is focused on pleasing you.

_____ My mental attention is focused on protecting you.

_____ My mental attention is focused on manipulating you to "do it my way."

_____ My self-esteem is bolstered by solving your problems.

_____ My self-esteem is bolstered by relieving your pain.

_____ My own hobbies and interests are put aside. My time is spent sharing your hobbies and interests.

_____ Your clothing and personal appearance are dictated by my desires because I feel you are a reflection of me.

_____ Your behavior is dictated by my desires because I feel you are a reflection of me.

_____ I am not aware of how I feel. I am aware of how you feel. I am not aware of what I want. I ask you what you want. If I am not aware of something, I assume.

_____ The dreams I have for my future are linked to you.

_____ My fear of rejection determines what I say or do.

____ My fear of your anger determines what I say or do.

____ I use giving as a way of feeling safe in our relationship.

____ My social circle diminishes as I involve myself with you.

____ I put my values aside in order to connect with you.

____ I value your opinion and way of doing things more than my own.

____ The quality of my life is in relation to the quality of yours.[3]

We should note here that the problem of codependency may take on an added dimension within religious circles where certain codependent traits have been mistakenly identified as positive "Christian" behavior. Some churches dangerously teach that it is a virtue to be constantly giving and sacrificing without receiving; that we must always put ourselves last with no thought of our own needs; and even that we must tolerate physical abuse from those we love. These ideas, of course, only parody true Scriptural teaching. Remember Christ's exhortation: We must love our neighbor *as* we love ourselves—not *more than* we love ourselves.

A long-term pattern of codependency will have its own tangled psychological roots of trauma, role models, cultural messages, and other influences. But these underlying causes of codependency can be dealt with successfully through support groups and professional care.

Other Roles That Don't Work

The notion of role-playing by people on the border of disorder received some attention in the early 1970s through the work of Claude M. Steiner, who wrote *Games Alcoholics Play*[4] and *Scripts People Live*[5]. Steiner explored the concept of the Karpman Drama Triangle, developed by Stephen B. Karpman. This triangle refers to a common pattern in which border people take on a triad of roles in

[3]Sandra Simpson LeSourd, *The Compulsive Woman* (Tarrytown, N.Y.: Chosen Books/Revell, 1987), p. 280.
[4]Claude M. Steiner, *Games Alcoholics Play* (New York: Grove Press, 1971).
[5]Steiner, *Scripts People Live* (New York: Grove Press, 1974).

relation to the disordered person—rescuer, persecutor, and victim. Beattie describes the process in simple terms: "We rescue people from their responsibilities. . . . Later we get mad at *them* for what *we've* done. Then we feel used and sorry for ourselves. That is the pattern, the triangle."[6]

We have found those three roles to clearly be among the many that border people assume. What kinds of roles have you played as you cope with the disordered person you love? Perhaps you can find yourself somewhere—even several places—in the following list. Keep in mind that any of these negative roles, if assumed repeatedly in multiple relationships, may indicate a codependent pattern that warrants its own therapeutic response.

The Enabler

The Enabler is a person whose means of helping are destructive. Actions that assist a disordered person to perpetuate inappropriate behavior, or prevent the person from suffering the consequences of such behavior, constitute enabling.

Enablers rescue disordered people from their responsibilities, doing for them what they should be doing for themselves. When the drug addict gets strung out and misses work, they call the boss to say she's "sick." When the alcoholic fails to make it home from the bar, they go looking for him, find him, and bring him home to bed.

A letter from the ex-wife of a compulsive gambler, published in a nationally syndicated advice column, describes the Enablers who surrounded the man and perpetuated his behavior:

> I was subjected to a lot of pain that could have been avoided if my husband's family had not rescued him every time he got into trouble. Over the years, they arranged loans for him, and when he couldn't pay up, they looked the other way while he stole money from them. When you try to cover up for a person who is addicted to gambling, you are doing him no favor. You

---

[6]Claude M. Steiner, *Games Alcoholics Play* (New York: Grove Press, 1971); Steiner, *Scripts People Live* (Grove, 1974); Beattie, p. 78.

are simply delaying the day of reckoning and putting him on a collision course with disaster.[7]

Enablers need to be needed. They keep disordered people needy by defending them, making excuses for them, cleaning up their messes, and lying to cover for them. Their help is really no help at all. In reality, they only help dig the pit deeper.

The People Pleaser

People Pleasers "help" the disordered person just as Enablers do. Yet while Enablers need to be needed, People Pleasers need to be liked. Rejection must be avoided at all costs, so they will pursue peace at any price. But the price they pay is too steep. They avoid rejection at the cost of the disordered person's health—and their own.

People Pleasers have trouble saying no to the disordered person even when they know they should. They say, "It doesn't matter," even when it really does. They seldom feel anger about their situation, but often feel hurt. They apologize often, avoid discussing the disorder to keep the peace, and would rather give in to the disordered person than risk that person's anger.[8]

We knew one wife who was aware that her husband was addicted to sleeping pills. She wanted him to break the habit, but she was terrified of his displeasure. So whenever he asked her to refill his prescription, she complied. She was a classic People Pleaser.

The Martyr

Martyrs believe they must sacrifice their own health and happiness—and that of others as well—for the sake of some worthy cause: to help the disordered person, to keep the family together, to protect a reputation. But in reality, these causes make no such absolute demands. The true, hidden cause Martyrs sacrifice so much for is their own sense of worth. They need to feel "noble," and martyrdom makes them feel that way.

Martyrs believe they were born to suffer, and that they

---

[7]Ann Landers column, *The Orlando Sentinel*, February 21, 1992, p. E–7.
[8]Adapted from *The Compulsive Woman*, p. 266.

must learn to "suffer well," as one Martyr we know described it. They endure and even indulge the disordered person as part of their "calling." When life goes smoothly for a while, they begin to anticipate disaster. When an opportunity for fun arises, their first impulse is to say no. Pain, they have concluded, is simply their lot in life.

Even so, you can be sure that on a regular basis Martyrs will inform the disordered person, and everyone else who will listen, just how much they have sacrificed. Their suffering must have an audience. The result: misery and self-righteousness on the part of the Martyr; more misery and resentment on the part of the disordered person.

The Savior

The Savior role is usually played by someone with a track record of success in solving problems. Saviors like to make things happen, find the answer, rescue the disordered person—and be recognized for their efforts. Confident that success will be theirs, they especially enjoy tackling what others consider an impossible situation.

Saviors love the limelight. They want to ride in on a white horse, save the day and receive the glory. Like the other negative roles, Saviors have a hidden agenda: They want to "help" so they can bolster their sense of self-esteem.

Consequently, when Saviors fail to fix a disordered person—as they inevitably do—they refuse to accept responsibility for the failure. They must assign blame, usually to the disordered person. That person must then wear a "black hat" so the Savior can continue to wear a "white hat."

Sometimes the Savior may even be a professional trying to treat a disorder. We know of some therapists who intentionally "wean" their clients from dependent relationships in the border network by encouraging dependence on themselves. The danger of that strategy is illustrated by a letter we once received from an anorexic woman who wrote:

> I put on enough weight so that you wouldn't call me skinny anymore. But I grew terribly dependent on

my psychiatrist. He was so loving and so patient with me through all of my ups and downs. Well, to everyone's shock he committed suicide a few days ago. Now I feel I've lost the only person in the whole world who fully understood my problem and could really offer me help.

The woman concluded by saying she could "already feel the panic setting in," and she feared finding another doctor to start all over again.

The Magician

Like Saviors, Magicians are expected to save the day when no one else can. But while the Savior is a self-chosen role, the Magician's role is usually assigned by someone else. The disordered person and the border network believe that someone with expertise—typically a counselor, therapist, or doctor—will work miracles.

"We've put aside our pride and emptied our bank account to become your client," they say to the psychiatrist. "Now we expect you to have all the answers and work wonders immediately." But Magicians can never meet such expectations because there is no such thing as magic—only the illusion of magic. Recovery is a process with no shortcuts, magical or otherwise.

What happens when Magicians fail to produce any "tricks"? They get blamed for the problem. The disordered person goes looking for another Magician, or worse yet, gives up seeking help altogether.

The Commander

Commanders believe the best and most direct way to overcome a disorder is to take charge of it themselves. They bark orders at the disordered person and everyone else in the border network, telling them how to shape up, confident that if everyone simply does what they say, everything will be fine.

The problem, of course, is that those who would be Commanders need an army—preferably a volunteer army—to execute their commands. But the disordered person and others as well, feeling coerced, will rebel against their orders, compromising their authority. Battle lines will be drawn, and the Commander simply will not win.

As the defeat grows obvious and the Commander recognizes that control has not been achieved, one of two reactions is common: The Commander either abdicates and withdraws in anger, or redoubles the effort by becoming a dictator. Both reactions only make matters worse.

The Enforcer

This role, usually received unwillingly by someone in the border network, is assigned by the Commander. Commanders declare martial laws that require Enforcers to carry them out.

When the Commander father of a drug-addicted daughter forbids her to see or even talk on the phone with her drug-abusing friends, he expects the other family members to become Enforcers of the rule. If they answer the door when her friends come by and Dad isn't home, they have to be the "heavy" who turns the friends away. If they catch her holding a forbidden phone conversation, they must turn informer or risk the father's wrath.

Enforcers are thus caught uncomfortably between the Commander's unilaterally issued laws and their own feelings about what an appropriate response to the problem might be. If Enforcers are made uncomfortable enough, they will join the disordered person in rebellion against the Commander.

The Worrier

People on the border quite naturally worry about the disordered person. But those who assume the role of Worrier make it their vocation. They believe that if they spend enough energy worrying, the situation will change. They feel irresponsible if they *don't* worry.

Worriers make futile statements to themselves like "I don't know what I'll do if . . ." This full-time agonizing would be bad enough even if it only agonized over the future. But Worriers also fret over the past. Their continual lament: "If only I had . . ." or "if only she had . . ."

Concern over a situation is fruitful if it motivates us to do something constructive or to learn from the past. But mere worry is sterile; it paralyzes us and emotionally exhausts us. Worse yet, if the worries are talked about regularly—and they usually are—they become a form of nagging, and the disordered person will grow resentful.

The Sampler

Samplers try to solve a disorder by trying a little of this and a little of that. Every remedy they hear about must be forced on the disordered person. Like a young child collecting shells on the beach, they grab every item that comes along. But each time they pick up a new one, they have to drop one they picked up before.

Sometimes Samplers take this role simply out of desperation. They believe they would be irresponsible if they didn't try everything, and they anxiously hope the next approach they try just might work. We have received letters from people on the border who fill ten pages with tiny handwriting to describe in detail all the strategies they have attempted.

Sometimes, however, the problem is that Samplers don't have the patience and perseverance to follow through with any one approach. There's nothing wrong with being eclectic in our strategy, but continual therapeutic "turnover" is confusing. In addition, Samplers usually fail to integrate the different therapies they adopt into a consistent, comprehensive plan. They end up instead with a therapeutic patchwork quilt, oddly shaped and full of holes.

Such an approach breeds not just confusion, but disillusionment. In time the Sampler concludes, "I've tried everything, but nothing works," and the disordered person may agree, giving up hope for recovery.

The Faddist

Faddists resemble Samplers in that they keep trying different methods. But while Samplers seek *variety*, Faddists are attracted to *novelty*. A Sampler may try out an ancient treatment like acupuncture, but the Faddist continually looks for the latest book, the latest tape, the latest speaker—the new "solution" that promises results no one else has ever achieved.

Like Samplers, Faddists haven't yet developed the tenacity required to stick with a particular treatment until it has time to work. Worse yet, the methods they attempt, like all fads, tend to be unproven, sensationalist, ungrounded, and reductionist. After all, fads grow popular quickly because they promise so much without requiring much of an investment of time, energy, money, or even careful thought. Therefore, the Faddist role leads only to futility and burnout.

The Spy

We discussed this role thoroughly in chapter 5, but we mention it here again as a reminder. Spies seek evidence to incriminate the disordered person; their agenda is to humiliate and punish the person while vindicating themselves. They go beyond gathering facts to set traps through deceit. The Spy role leads only to mutual mistrust and lower self-esteem in the disordered person—which only intensify the destructive behavior.

The Paramedic

This role was noted earlier as well. Paramedics conclude that since they live on the scene of an emergency, they must take drastic measures to save the disordered person's life. Like an emergency medic pounding the chest of a cardiac arrest victim or applying electrodes, they treat the person harshly, trying a kind of "shock" therapy.

Paramedics often go beyond abusive words to actual physical violence. We once spoke to an acquaintance who confessed that he grew so desperate over his wife's anorexia that he tried to force food down her throat and knocked her around the room with his fist to "jolt her into reality." His behavior was totally inappropriate, and it only succeeded in bruising and terrifying his wife. As with most Paramedics, anger lay beneath his violence; his harshness was motivated by a desire to punish rather than to heal.

The Shuttle Diplomat

Diplomacy is generally a good thing, and most border networks have at least one member who acts at times as a helpful mediator between the disordered person and the others. This diplomatic activity helps the person and strengthens the network if it clarifies positions, clears up misunderstandings, and allows those involved to build bridges of empathy and compassion.

The mediator role becomes dysfunctional, however, when the person playing it turns into what we call a Shuttle Diplomat. Shuttle Diplomats incessantly run back and forth between conflicting parties to try to make everyone happy. Rather than trying to work themselves out of a job by bringing people together, they enjoy the role of go-between. It's a position of power they view as continual, permanent, and indispensable to the network.

Much news has been made by American Secretary of State James Baker, who has brought Israel and several Arab nations together for peace talks. His many trips between national capitals were critical in helping the parties come to a mutual understanding of positions, and, apparently, he has accomplished much good. But his ultimate mission was not to create a permanent shuttling job; the goal was rather to bring the warring parties to the same table so they themselves can resolve their differences.

The same is true for mediators in the border network. Their mission is to get people in conflict together so they can come to an agreement, or at least a truce. But the self-perpetuated role of the Shuttle Diplomat short-circuits that process. Instead of clearing the airwaves for communication, it only perpetuates the conflict by keeping others dependent on its own perpetual mediation.

Shuttle Diplomats may succeed at remaining indispensable in the eyes of the border network. But if they also hope to keep everyone happy, they will find that goal unattainable. Sooner or later, even Shuttle Diplomats discover that they can't guarantee the happiness of other people.

The roles we have just described are dysfunctional because they operate on the same faulty assumption that underlies quick fixes: *They assume we can ultimately control other people's choices and take responsibility for their happiness.*

What's the alternative? Becoming a genuine "supporting cast" for the disordered person.

12

Positive Roles and Personality Types

—Cherry and Dan

The idea of *relational therapy* was introduced in chapter 3 as the third element in a comprehensive approach to recovery. We said that relationships in the border network have the potential to minister healing to the disordered person at the deep level where self-esteem has been wounded and maladaptive responses have been generated.

In short, we concluded, if you can provide a disordered person with genuine love, honesty, and empathy, you can be that person's best therapy. This insight is confirmed by the work of psychotherapist Carl Rogers, whose concept of the therapeutic personality is based on his conclusion that professional helpers' theoretical orientation is not as important as whether they possess certain personal qualities. He described these traits as unconditional positive regard (what we would call love), genuineness (honesty), and compassion (empathy).[1]

Love, we said, is a condition that exists when another person's well-being and security are as important to you as your own. Empathy, we noted, has remarkable power to heal, a quality demonstrated even in clinical experiments. Honesty, as we observed in our discussion of denial, discernment, deceit, and disclosure, is indispensable for progress toward recovery.

---

[1]Carl Rogers, *On Becoming a Person* (Boston: Houghton-Mifflin, 1961), pp. 39–58.

In light of those insights, we now want to identify several roles that demonstrate to the disordered person a posture of love, empathy, and honesty. Though some people in the border network will be better at one than another, ideally everyone who desires to join the healing community should seek to take on all these roles as the opportunity arises.

The Nurturer

The literal meaning of the word *nurturer* is "one who feeds." But what part of the disordered person are we to feed?

What people with an impulse control disorder need most is nourishment for their *self-esteem*. Life experiences of one sort or another have diminished their feelings of worth, and the failure to overcome the disorder has only compounded the problem. To regain a sense of personal value, they need the repeated, loving affirmation of others whose approval counts.

Not surprisingly, these "significant others" will most likely be found in the border network. More than anyone else, family members, close friends, and respected figures such as a pastor or doctor stand in a powerful position. If they persistently send to the disordered person a simple message—"You are valuable"—in time the person will begin to believe what they say.

Richard and Reneé Durfield, in their book *Raising Them Chaste*, identify three "building blocks" of self-esteem we would do well to keep in mind:

- *a sense of importance*—a conviction that we are significant, that our life matters.
- *a sense of belonging*—a conviction that we have a place in the world where we fit, where we are welcome, and where we are accepted.
- *a sense of ability*—a conviction that we are competent and can make a contribution to the world.[2]

Nurturing these three convictions in a seriously disordered person will be a challenge. Their disorder has left

---

[2]Richard C. Durfield, Ph.D. and Reneé Durfield, *Raising Them Chaste* (Minneapolis: Bethany House Publishers, 1991), pp. 119–125.

them feeling just the opposite: insignificant, alienated, and incompetent. Yet we can communicate our esteem for them through the three everyday channels of attitudes, words, and behavior.

To build someone's self-esteem, our attitude must convey above all a solid *respect*. How do we approach the disordered person's feelings, opinions, beliefs, and decisions? Do we recognize them as worthwhile even when we don't share them?

Our words have the power to heal or destroy. People with low-self esteem often were raised in an atmosphere of verbal criticism, complaint, and condemnation. Those explicitly negative messages must now be countered by our consistent words of sincere *praise*. We must be on the alert for even the smallest occasions to express affirmation.

Psychologists have long been aware that human beings deprived of *physical affection* suffer emotional damage. On the other hand, hugs, gentle pats, an arm around the shoulder, and other appropriate natural ways of touching a disordered person can powerfully convey the sense of connectedness and belonging necessary for self esteem.

These are only three of many elements in a relationship that communicate esteem, but they are essential. If we patiently and persistently provide them as a steady emotional diet for the disordered person, we will gradually nurture the person's self-image back to health.

The Co-Sufferer

If empathy is foundational for healing relationships, people on the border must be willing to identify with the suffering and struggle of the disordered person. Recognizing that suffering can be redemptive, they can help bear the person's burdens—and a burden shared is only half as heavy. This is the primary value of mutual support groups like Alcoholics Anonymous and Weight Watchers.

Sometimes empathy will be expressed by a simple gesture such as sharing a "good cry" together. To empathize most accurately, however, we need to grasp thoroughly what is going on inside the disordered person, appreciating the pain and frustration, the confusion and the bondage. We must understand not only the person's thoughts, feelings, and perceptions, but even the bio-chemical conditions that contribute to depression and other problems.

This involves investing some time in study and dis-cussion of the disorder's sources, symptoms, and cure. It also requires the cultivation of active listening skills so that we can fully receive what the disordered person has to tell us.

The Partner

Like the Co-Sufferer, the Partner comes alongside the disordered person. But the Partner focuses less on the pain and struggle and more on the task of healing to be accomplished. Partners get in the "yoke" with the disor-dered person to share the hard work of recovery.

Partners don't need the glory that the Savior role seeks. They don't desire the controlling power of the Commander. Nor do they see themselves as Magicians with all the answers.

Instead, Partners want to cooperate with the disor-dered person's own decisions to progress toward recov-ery. They recognize that they are only one of many con-tributors to healing. They know the value of community, and they are happy to be a player on the therapeutic team.

The Witness

Impulse control disorders can generate such intense negative feelings in the border network that its members have difficulty seeing the situation objectively. They have developed a pattern of reacting to the disordered person with anger or fear rather than insight. Dr. Ray Vath notes that one of his major challenges is to recruit these "emo-tional reactionaries" for a new role in the healing com-munity as Witnesses.

Witnesses are border people willing to "bear witness" to the disordered person's experiences and choices, and their consequences. For example, when the person feels depressed, Witnesses don't react with such emotional ac-cusation as "You just enjoy feeling bad!" Instead they look for patterns that reveal helpful insights: "You know, when the doctor puts you on that medication, it seems to help you a great deal. But when you stop taking it, I notice that you get depressed rather quickly."

While the role of Spy watches intently to catch the disordered person failing, Witnesses cultivate their skills of observation to enhance the healing process. They notice what works and what doesn't. Then they reflect that information back to the disordered person and the rest of the therapeutic team, not as informers but as faithful encouragers who want the plan of recovery to be shaped by accurate feedback.

The Enlightener

As we noted in chapter 3, cognitive therapy recognizes that knowledge is power, and self-knowledge in particular can catalyze personal transformation. While the Nurturer, Co-Sufferer, and Partner play major roles in relational therapy, the Witness and Enlightener contribute to cognitive therapy.

Enlighteners carefully examine the information provided by the disordered person, the border network and their own training and experience. They integrate this information into a bigger picture that will yield useful insights. Unlike Saviors, Commanders and Paramedics, Enlighteners recognize that they can't rescue disordered people, make their choices for them, or force them to "straighten out." Instead, they see their role as one of *illumination* and *clarification*.

Choosing their words carefully, Enlighteners craft questions that will draw fresh insights out of the disordered person. Then, in the light of those newly discovered truths, they go on to clarify the choices facing the person and the consequences of each choice. Dr. Vath is a master of this role and has employed this technique with great success.

At the urging of his wife, Debbie, a man named Steve who was a successful businessman in the Seattle area, made an appointment with Dr. Vath to discuss his cocaine habit. He went under protest, explaining to Dr. Vath, "I'm in control—I frankly would just like to get my wife off my back." An interesting conversation followed:

Dr. Vath: You seem to be quite a success—I see by your resume that you've started and built up six businesses.

Steve: You could say that. Yes, I've pretty much accomplished everything I set out to do.

Dr. Vath: The proverbial self-made man . . .

Steve: Yeah, I guess you could say that—I've made my own way in life and managed pretty well. Since childhood, actually.

Dr. Vath: Pulled yourself up by your own bootstraps.

Steve: I suppose so, yes.

Dr. Vath: Great looking pair of boots you're wearing, by the way. How long did it take you to make them?

Steve: *(puzzled)* What? Make them? I bought them in Italy.

Dr. Vath: Oh, I see. Well, do you think you could have made a pair of boots like that?

Steve: I suppose not. No. I wouldn't know how.

Dr. Vath: And that Rolex watch—a beautiful timepiece. Think you could design and assemble one of those?

Steve: C'mon! Where are you taking me with this?

Dr. Vath: Seems to me you may have needed other people—bootmakers, watchmakers—in your life. And many more, if we really think about it. None of us can really manage alone. We're social creatures. We need one another's help.

Steve: I've never really thought about it that way, but, yes, I see your point.

Dr. Vath: As long as you feel you don't really need others, Steve, you will not acknowledge that it will take help to stop your cocaine use.

Steve: I'm not an addict.

Dr. Vath: But certainly you're aware of the possible health consequences.

Steve: I'm not a heavy user—it's more recreational with me.

Dr. Vath: You could be arrested—lose your business.

Pretty high price for recreation, wouldn't you say?

Steve: O.K. Let's talk.

This fascinating session between therapist and patient illustrates several points. As Enlightener, Ray Vath feeds back Steve's self-sufficient attitude and gently destroys it with a simple illustration. Steve needs others. Until he acknowledges this truth, he is doomed to believe he can "quit coke anytime." Dr. Vath, without condemnation, then clarifies the issue further by posing possible consequences for Steve's cocaine use, which are severe and sobering. By gently casting light on Steve's false sense of self-sufficiency and by illuminating potential disaster, the therapist successfully persuades Steve to admit his need for help and consider treatment—all in one session.

The Empowerer

Nurturers feed self-esteem so disordered people will want to choose life and freedom. Enlighteners offer insights to clarify that choice and its consequences. But Empowerers provide the tools to carry out the choice effectively.

What are those tools? Empowerers point people toward concrete approaches to recovery. They offer practical therapeutic strategies such as how to develop communication skills, how to self-monitor feelings, and how to discern the effects of various medications. They connect people to mutual support groups, public agencies, and other resources that can supplement the contributions of the border network.

Most of all, Empowerers offer hope. They cheer disordered people along, remind them frequently that healing is possible, provide examples of others who have won the struggle and say in countless ways, "I believe in you. You can do it." Empowerers know that hope is a potent motivator that will pull hurting people into a healthy future.

These six roles—Nurturer, Co-Sufferer, Partner, Witness, Enlightener and Empowerer—by no means exhaust the range of relational postures that can contribute to healing. But they are, nonetheless, essential parts to be played in the very real drama of comprehensive recovery strategies. Taken together, these roles embody the powerful traits and potential of the therapeutic personality: love, honesty, and empathy.

Roles and Personality Types

For at least twenty-five hundred years, people have tried to categorize the human temperament according to basic, distinctive ways of relating to the world. In the fifth century B.C. the Greek physician Hippocrates, known as the father of medical science, divided humanity into four personality types: Sanguine, Choleric, Phlegmatic, and Melancholic. This fourfold division remained the traditional theory in the Western world until Carl Jung published his system of eight categories in 1920.

Since then, other schemes have attempted to build on this classification, most notably the Myers-Briggs Type Indicator published by Katherine C. Briggs and Isabel Briggs Myers in 1962. A few years later clinical psychologist David Keirsey, who adapted the insights of the Myers-Briggs research to describe the four basic types in new terms, labelled them the Epimethean, Dionysian, Promethean, and Apollonian personalities.[3]

We found Keirsey's insights especially helpful in our efforts to understand each other and to cooperate in the process of my recovery. Since a healing community must be characterized by empathy, we recommend that people in the border network make use of a personality test such as the Keirsey Temperament Sorter presented in the book *Please Understand Me* by David Keirsey and Marilyn Bates[4] Such tests help us discover basic temperamental differences between us and those we love, freeing us to recognize them as legitimate variations in human nature. When we appreciate the full range of human tempera-

---

[3]Chester P. Michael, Marie C. Norrisey, *Prayer and Temperament: Different Prayer Forms for Different Personality Types* (Charlottesville, Va.: The Open Door, Inc., 1984), pp. 11–12, 16.

[4]David Keirsey and Marilyn Bates, *Please Understand Me* (Del Mar, Calif.: Prometheus Nemesis Books, 1978).

ments, we are less likely to impose our own ways of viewing the world on others.[5]

We note the usefulness of personality testing in this chapter because we suspect that different temperamental types may tend toward different roles in the border network. Though we are aware of no research to confirm our premonitions, our experience suggests that the weaknesses of each personality type can make a person vulnerable to certain negative roles we have previously described. On the other hand, the strengths of the same type can become a valuable asset in cultivating one or more of the positive roles.

What Keirsey calls the Dionysian type, for example, tends toward impulsive behavior. So we might well find that Dionysians are tempted to take the roles of Sampler and Faddist. Keirsey's Promethean type, on the other hand, tends toward rigid control of situations—and thus might find the roles of Commander or Paramedic attractive.

The Epimethean wants to be a caretaker and often acts as a parent to other adults. This type would easily fall into the roles of the Enabler and the Shuttle Diplomat. Meanwhile, the Apollonian, who persistently seeks a meaningful mission in life and thrives on recognition, would find the roles of Savior and Martyr a comfortable fit.

We see a correspondence between temperamental strengths and positive roles as well. The Prometheans' natural mastery of information make them good candidates for Witnesses and Enlighteners. The Apollonians' strong optimism and empathy make them natural Nurturers and Co-Sufferers. The Dionysians' cheerfulness and emphasis on action serve well in the role of Empowerer. And the team spirit and stability of Epimetheans would allow them to become excellent Partners.

These correlations between roles and personality types are meant to be suggestive rather than conclusive. We recognize that the human psyche is so complex, no system of classification is fully adequate to describe or predict its patterns. In addition, though some roles may seem to

---

[5]Keirsey and Bates, pp. 5–13, 27–66.

have affinities with certain temperaments, our temperament type certainly doesn't *limit* us to those roles. Circumstances can push people into negative roles they
might otherwise avoid, and we should cultivate *all* the
positive roles as much as possible—even those that don't
seem to come naturally.

Even so, any insights we can gain from understanding
personality differences among the people involved with
an impulse control disorder will foster mutual empathy,
understanding, and tolerance. Combined with an awareness of the roles people on the border play, this kind of
knowledge holds healing power—and the potential for
cultivating healthier relationships in every area of our
lives.

13

Giving Up

—Dan

The first of the famous "Twelve Steps" of Alcoholics Anonymous, adopted by many other mutual support groups as well, begins: "We admit that we are powerless over people, places, and circumstances . . ." That is a painful, humbling admission, and yet a necessary key to health—not only for the disordered person, but for the border network as well.

We want to believe we have power over our lives because we fear being out of control. We want to believe we have at least a measure of power over the people close to us because their behavior affects our lives profoundly. We fear that if the people close to us are out of control, our lives will also spin out of control. This is precisely why we are so threatened by living on the border of disorder.

The middle term of the phrase "impulse control disorder" thus identifies the issue that lies in the middle of the disordered dilemma. *Control* is what most disordered people desperately desire, what they persistently lack, and what their loved ones insistently try to supply. When all is said and done, disordered people are battling for *control*, fighting against their past, their culture, their own splintered will, sometimes their own body chemistry. And in most cases, sadly enough, they are also fighting against those of us on the border.

That battle is by no means one-sided. A good deal of this book has, in fact, been devoted to identifying the myriad ways in which the border network fights for control with its own largely ineffective and frequently destructive weapons: quick fixes, backlash, bargaining, "911 approaches," and negative roles. The truth of the "First Step" remains: *We are powerless over people.*

Ironically, almost all people with impulse control disorders try sooner or later to find someone who will stop them from their self-destruction. Police records show that even serial offenders—those who struggle with compulsive criminal behavior—sometimes write letters to the police asking the law to stop them before they commit another crime. One part of the disordered person's will is pleading, "Will you control this thing I can't control? Will you stop me from destroying myself?" Yet the other part of the person's will wins out. Even when we try to provide the needed control through coercion, manipulation or bargaining, it fails to work.

In the final analysis, we have no power to make other people's choices for them. As Dr. Vath says, "In the end they will do what they will do and I will do what I will do." Nor can we guarantee other people's happiness. My friend Dan Ganfield, who with his wife, Chrissie, became significant members of our healing community in Seattle, puts it this way: "Ultimately, people are free to choose their own blues."

When we *do* try to determine others' choices, we cause interior problems for ourselves—specifically, we experience what clinical psychologist Lawrence Crabb calls "Basic Anxiety." That anxiety is the sense of frustration and apprehension that necessarily results when we set out to control what we cannot control. Crabb notes as well that when we don't succeed in such efforts, we develop a sense of *false guilt*, which he describes as "the result of failing to reach an unreachable goal."[1]

Any strategy to control others is thus doomed to failure. So how do we cope if we can't control the people who bring such chaos into our lives?

The answer is simple, though not easy: *We give up.*

---

[1]Lawrence J. Crabb, Jr., *Inside Out* (Colorado Springs: NavPress, 1988), pp. 141–143.

The Wrong Way to Give Up

What do we mean when we say "give up"? Let's talk first about what we *don't* mean.

By giving up, we don't mean *giving up the relationship*. Abandoning the disordered person may provide us with some temporary relief, but ultimately it may cause more problems than it solves, especially if it means breaking up a family and separating children from a parent. This measure should only be taken in such extreme cases as a physically abusive relationship, where someone's health and safety are at stake.

As we noted in chapter 10, disengagement from family or the local environment for a period of time can sometimes prove helpful in recovery. But giving up on the disordered person altogether—cutting off the relationship and checking out permanently—tears a hole in the fabric of the healing community and pushes the person further toward despair.

We once received a letter from a husband who was on the verge of abandoning his anorexic/bulimic wife. He wrote:

> We have been married three years, but the way things are going, divorce is a real possibility. I moved out last week. Shirley is anorexic and bulimic. In recent months, she has lost so much weight that she has not been able to work, and she will rarely take my advice even though she acknowledges the fact that I know a fair amount about fitness and nutrition. When we got married, I thought we could handle her eating (or non-eating) problems together, but it has proven to be too much for me.

We certainly understood this man's exasperation; the situation sounded all too familiar. Yet we also knew that even though our own marriage at one time had been just as fragile, we survived together. We wrote back: "Don't let go! What Shirley needs now, more than ever, is support, acceptance, and love."

The second thing we don't mean when we say "give up" is giving up on *restoring order to our own lives*. Giving up is not a cold, hostile withdrawal from reality in which we resign ourselves to putting up with whatever happens. Where the disordered behavior has devastated our life, we must draw some boundaries to protect ourselves. We must manage our own physical, financial, emotional, and spiritual well-being, doing what is necessary to love ourselves as much as we love our neighbor.

Members of the border network aren't the only ones guilty of trying to control others. The inappropriate behavior of disordered people becomes a tool of manipulation as well, entangling those in the border network and pulling their "strings." But to permit such control only perpetuates the problem.

We have to say, "My life counts too, and I have to go on living." We begin to reclaim our lives from the chaos. In a sense, we must define a healthy zone of "space" around the disordered person that has clear inner and outer boundaries. We don't want to create such distance that we abandon the person. But neither do we want to move so close in that we get sucked into the manipulation of the disordered behavior.

Most importantly, giving up does not mean *giving up hope*. Hope is as essential to recovery as love, honesty, and empathy—perhaps even more. Without hope we lose the motivational "anchor" of our souls, the quality that empowers us to hold steady and survive when the waves of tumultuous circumstances break around us and look their worst.

Jerome Frank, in an essay on the role of hope in psychotherapy, defines hopelessness as *the inability to imagine a tolerable future*.[2] Those who lose hope conclude that they simply cannot bear whatever tomorrow will bring. No wonder, then, that extreme hopelessness (a form of depression) can be life-threatening.

Some people without hope simply commit suicide; at least sixty people in our country make that choice every day.[3] Others lose the will to live and soon after succumb

---

[2]Jerome Frank, "The Role of Hope in Psychotherapy," *International Journal of Psychiatry*: Vol. 5 (1968), pp. 383–95.
[3]Sandra Simpson LeSourd, *The Compulsive Woman* (Tarrytown, N.Y.: Chosen Books/Revell, 1990), p. 297.

to an illness, an accident, or "old age." As is often noted by those whose loved ones have died in nursing homes, just prior to death many patients simply give up on life.

Leo Thomas and Jan Alkire of the Institute for Christian Ministries tell the story of an elderly woman named Myrtle. When a flu kept her in bed at a nursing home for several months, she lost her ability to walk. But she was determined to be on her feet again, so she exercised her legs in bed and hounded her aides to help her walk. The recovery was slow, but she eventually learned to walk again with a cane, left the nursing home, and lived alone again—for ten more years.

Then Myrtle broke her hip and ended up in the nursing home once more. But this time the staff refused to help her learn to walk again. They said the effort would be a waste of time, and her doctor told her: "You are 93 years old. You are too old and weak; you will never walk again."

After he left, Myrtle told her friend, "I'm going to die. There is no sense in living now." Within three weeks she was dead, "killed by a lethal dose of hopelessness."[4]

At times during Cherry's long recovery, I must admit that I myself came perilously close to hopelessness. Though I never contemplated taking my own life directly, when things were at their worst I sometimes jeopardized my safety by riding my motorcycle far too fast on dangerous roads—at least subconsciously open to the possibility that an accident might allow me to escape it all. Somehow that seemed to be the only honorable way out, but of course it would have solved nothing.

Hopelessness can be threatening to our interior lives as well. So we must always cling to hope, even if only a little. Dr. Paul Pruyser, a collaborator with Dr. Karl Menninger, once concluded: "One little ray [of hope] is enough to invigorate some people. One moment of release from unbearable stress makes the world appear in a different image."[5]

[4]Leo Thomas, O.P. and Jan Alkire, *Healing as a Parish Ministry* (Notre Dame, Ind.: Ave Maria Press, 1992), p. 136–147.
[5]Paul Pruyser, "The Phenomenology and Dynamics of Hoping," *The Journal of the Scientific Study of Religion*: Vol. 3 (1963), pp. 93–94.

Giving Up the Right Way

What is the right way to give up? Ultimately, the right kind of giving up is a *renunciation of our attempts to control the disordered situation and to surrender that situation*. But few of us will find this kind of surrender easy.

One obstacle we encounter is our pride. To give up is a humbling experience: We must admit our limitations, our creatureliness, our dependence on grace. We come to recognize that we don't have all the answers, and that even if we did, healing still would not depend on us.

A second obstacle is our fear. We are afraid of what the outcome of the situation might be if we let go. We feel, as it were, as though we are flying blind—about to impact a mountainside. We confront our powerlessness and find it truly horrifying—until we recognize that power was only an illusion in the first place.

If we learn anything from living on the border of disorder, it must be at least this much: We human beings are blessed with a free will, influenced though it may be by the forces of nature and nurture. We may abuse our freedom; we may twist our will in a hundred perverse directions, destroying our health and sanity and threatening the health and sanity of others. But in the end, we alone can choose brokenness or wholeness, misery or happiness, right or wrong.

This is not to say that we give up on offering help to troubled persons. We cannot cut the lifeline—but we must certainly cut the umbilical cord. Melodie Beattie describes it this way:

> We adopt a policy of keeping our hands off other people's responsibilities and tend to our own instead. If people have created some disasters for themselves, we allow them to face their own proverbial music. We allow people to be who they are. We give them the freedom to be responsible and grow. And we give ourselves that same freedom. We live our own lives to the best of our ability. We strive to ascertain what it is we can change and what we cannot change. Then we stop trying to change things we can't. We do what we can to solve a problem, and then we stop fretting

and stewing. If we cannot solve a problem and have done what we could, we learn to live with, or in spite of, that problem. And we try to live happily—focusing heroically on what is good in our lives today, and feeling grateful for that.[6]

In a word, we learn *acceptance*—what Elisabeth Kubler-Ross identified as the final stage in the process of grief.[7]

Even Parents Must Let Go

Letting go is perhaps hardest when the someone we must let go of is our son or daughter. Our first job as parents is to take care of our children, setting limits, making decisions for them they cannot yet make for themselves, bearing responsibilities they are unable to bear. Even though our ultimate goal is preparing them to do all these things on their own, we often second-guess ourselves, wondering whether we have released aspects of their lives too soon, hoping they won't stumble too often or too painfully when at last we let go of their hand and let them walk alone.

When the child we labored so lovingly to protect and encourage falls into an impulse control disorder, our hearts break. Maybe, we think, we didn't do enough—so we need to do it now. Maybe our son or daughter's childhood isn't really over yet, so we need to reassert control, take the hand again, wipe the nose, clean up the mess left behind.

Not long ago we met a father—we'll call him "Wayne"—who found himself in this very dilemma. We first heard from him in an overnight letter received via our publisher. Wayne had read Cherry's book *Starving for Attention*, and desperately wanted our help for his married, twenty-four-year-old daughter, Jessica, who was in the hospital starving from anorexia.

Wayne is a lieutenant on the police force of a major

---

[6]Melody, Beattie, *Codependent No More* (San Francisco: Harper/Hazelden, 1987), p. 56.
[7]Elisabeth Kubler-Ross, *On Death and Dying* (New York: Macmillan, 1969), pp. 112–137.

city, a man who exudes a sense of confidence and power. It was readily apparent that he was accustomed to being in control. Wayne insisted that we call his daughter in the hospital and tell her what to do.

In spite of the young woman's desperate situation, we had to politely decline to talk with her unless she contacted us herself. If she had been a minor, things might have been different. But she was refusing to call us on her own, and, as strangers, to forcefully intervene in the life of a married adult was inappropriate and would only exacerbate the problem.

That position seemed unreasonable to Wayne. We realized, however, that he was the kind of parent who had long found it difficult to relinquish control, even before the disorder emerged. If we allowed him to arrange the conversation and push his daughter into it, we would be affirming his mistaken conviction that he could overpower her and manipulate circumstances to control her. So we stood our ground.

Not surprisingly, Wayne persisted as well. He mailed registered letters to our home, sent us gifts, and even talked an unsuspecting friend of ours into giving him our unlisted phone number. Once the repeated phone calls began, I had to have a long, frank, and painful talk with the man.

"Look, Wayne," I said, "I recognize that you're a well-meaning father who loves his daughter very much and wants the best for her. But being in law enforcement, you also come across a bit like a drill sergeant who expects obedience to your every command. When you try to control Jessica's life this way, you only leave her one option: to continue her battle for control in the one area she can claim—her own body."

I explained to Wayne that he only made matters worse when he allowed his desperation to drive him to take charge of her life. I insisted that we could only help her when she herself chose to seek our help. Knowing his pain, I couldn't easily say what needed to be said: "Give up and let go." But I did.

Wayne took my words to heart and backed off. Within weeks Jessica finally called us on her own terms. At last we were in a position to help, and we have learned since then that our conversation made a positive difference.

A Checklist for Letting Go

What it means for the border network to give up, to let go, is summarized well by Sandra LeSourd. We can think of her insights as a checklist for our own attitudes as we seek to give up appropriately:

To "let go" does not mean to stop caring, but that I can't do it for someone else.

To "let go" is not to cut myself off, but to realize that I can't control another [person].

To "let go" is not to enable, but to allow learning from natural consequences.

To "let go" is to admit powerlessness, which means the outcome is not in my hands.

To "let go" is not to try to change or blame another, but to make the most of myself.

To "let go" is not to care for, but to care about.

To "let go" is not to fix, but to be supportive.

To "let go" is not to judge, but to allow another [person] to be a human being.

To "let go" is not to be in the middle arranging all the outcomes, but to allow others to affect their destinies.

To "let go" is not to be protective, but to permit another [person] to face reality.

To "let go" is not to deny, but to accept.

To "let go" is not to nag, scold or argue, but instead to search out my own shortcomings and correct them.

To "let go" is not to adjust everything to my desires, but to take each day as it comes, and cherish myself in it.

To "let go" is not to criticize and regulate anybody, but to try to become what I dream I can be.

To "let go" is not to regret the past, but to grow and live for the future.

To "let go" is to fear less, and love more.[8]

---

[8]LeSourd, p. 281.

Obviously, we can't let go in all these areas simultaneously. Our giving up, like our loved one's recovery, is an incremental process that takes time. Many days we will be tempted to seize control again. But each time we successfully surrender another matter, the next surrender comes more easily.

As an aid in the process, I recommend reading *Abandonment to Divine Providence* by Jean Pierre DeCaussade.[9] This powerful book provides simple yet profound insights that carry the potential of revolutionizing our view of how to let go in a positive and life-giving way.

As we give up, we aren't abandoning the disordered person, the situation, or ourselves. But we are abandoning a weight that's too great to carry—responsibility for another person's health and happiness. Once we surrender that impossible burden, we can receive in its place some precious gifts: freedom, humility, wisdom, and an abiding peace.

---

[9]Jean Pierre DeCaussade, *Abandonment to Divine Providence* (New York: Doubleday, 1975).

14

The Tunnel That Leads to the Light

—Dan and Cherry

One night while we were living with Dan's parents just after our move to Seattle, we had a family conference to discuss Cherry's situation. Like most people at the time, Bill—Dan's father—knew very little about anorexia or bulimia. But he spoke a few words that illuminated Cherry's struggle as few things had before that night.

He shared a simple thought: "One day at a time." Those were significant words because Cherry had always taken the all-or-nothing approach. In her eyes, anything less than total victory in this matter was defeat. But Bill's brief word of advice, offered in a spirit of unconditional love, revolutionized her thinking.

One day at a time. These words of wisdom are needed by the border network as much as the disordered person. If it took years for a disorder to develop, it will most likely take years for it to be overcome. Healing is a slow and incremental process, with many small victories and defeats. If we take the extremist "all or nothing" attitude, we'll end up with "nothing" every time. Recovery must be viewed as a long tunnel that eventually leads to the light.

When toddlers make their first attempts to walk, we don't criticize them because they fail to go from crawling to running in one day. Instead, we work patiently with them, encouraging every effort, applauding every step and offering comfort every time they fall. Recovery should be approached in much the same way. We must learn to celebrate the little steps of progress and extend a hand when our loved one stumbles.

We have often warned the anorexics who seek our advice not to gain back all their weight in a hurry. Besides being physically dangerous—the heart is a muscle weakened by starvation, and it can be overwhelmed by sudden increased demands on its labor—we've found that people who gain weight rapidly tend to panic and revert back to their old anorexic habits. Unless someone's weight is so low her life is threatened, we encourage her to take it slowly and steadily, and we tell her border network not to try to accelerate the process.

"One day at a time" applies not just to changing problem behavior but to every aspect of life on the border. We face our medical bills one day at a time. We rebuild trust one day at a time. We forgive, pray, resolve conflicts, cultivate new ways of relating all one day at a time. Above all, each new day we focus on even the smallest of indicators that progress is being made, appreciating them for the rays of hope they provide.

Signs of Recovery

How do we know when recovery is taking place? The obvious indication is a lessening of the disordered behavior. But as we've seen, true recovery must also include a resolution of underlying problems such as fear, low self-esteem, perfectionism, and misperceptions about how to cope with life.

Dr. Kim Lampson Reiff, a recovered bulimic and therapist we have known for many years, has developed a list of criteria for recovery that serves as a reference of indicators to border people who are observing the healing process. Although this abbreviated list of characteristics was intended to describe recovery from eating disorders, we believe it broadly applies to impulse control disorders in general. Here are the signs to look for:

1. *Acceptance of self and others.*

One indication of emotional health is the ability to recognize and accept human imperfection. Unrealistically high performance standards no longer determine self-worth. People are seen as a mixture of strengths and weaknesses that lead to successes and failures. Recovering people learn to rejoice over their accomplishments and victories, as well as those of others. They also learn to comfort others in failure and to receive comfort when they themselves fail.

2. *Love of self and others.*

The source of self-esteem shifts from external to internal qualities, from performance and achievement to love, honesty, and compassion in relationships. These latter traits are viewed not as rules to be obeyed but as goals to be strived for.

3. *Appropriate manliness or womanliness.*

Confused sexual identity plays a role in many serious behavioral disorders. One goal of recovery is to develop a positive, comfortable, functional concept of personal sexual identity and of sexuality in general.

4. *Joy.*

Depression should be significantly relieved so that as a whole the recovering person has vitality and a reasonable sense of joy about life. Also necessary is the resilience to tolerate the occasional "down" days that everyone experiences.

5. *Open honesty.*

As self-acceptance grows, recovering people grow comfortable and confident in sharing their successes with humility and their failures without shame. They seek out people who can respond with loving honesty and develop close, lasting relationships built on trust.

6. *Independence.*

By this, of course, we don't mean a proud or fearful isolation that refuses help from others. A healthy independence depends on a sense of personal competence to cope with problems. No longer does the person merely seek answers for specific questions, but wisdom for life as a whole. Wisdom leads recovering people to a self-directed autonomy that can overcome many challenges rather than a pursuit of questions that leaves them dependent on authority figures for their continued well-being. Opinions of others are considered carefully, but they are also evaluated, tested, and then incorporated into life when they prove to be valid and helpful.

7. Collaboration.

As a result of all these emerging traits, recovering people are able to take a self-assured approach to life. They can negotiate openly, freely, and confidently with others. They view the border network and others as cooperating partners rather than intimidating threats.

When these qualities are present to a reasonable degree and have become a solid part of the recovering person's character, the disorder has been conquered. Even if relapses occur, the basis for enduring health will be built and will prove to outlast any temporary recurrences of the problem.[1] A more detailed exploration of indicators of recovery, the best yet compiled in our opinion, is found in *Eating Disorders: Nutrition Therapy in the Recovery Process* by Dan W. Reiff, MPH, RD, and Kathleen Kim Lampson Reiff, Ph.D.[2]

Bumps in the Road

Even as the signs of recovery appear, we encounter a number of "bumps in the road" on the way to health. These are to be expected. The recovering person will stumble some days, and on other days surprise or puzzle us. Here are some challenges to prepare for:

---

[1]Raymond E. Vath, M.D., *Counseling Those With Eating Disorders* (Waco, Tex.: Word Publishing, 1986), pp. 182–184.
[2]Dan W. Reiff, MPH, RD, and Kathleen Kim Lampson Reiff, Ph.D., *Eating Disorders: Nutrition Therapy in the Recovery Process* (Gaithersburg, Md: Aspen Publishers, Inc., 1992), pp. 463–496.

When medication is no longer required.

In cases where a recovering person is being weaned from mood-stabilizing medication, you can expect some mood swings and inconsistent behavior. Use this time to develop your role as Witness, helping the person and the doctor chart mood patterns and problems. Recovering people need time to learn how to read their own symptoms so they can avoid emotional crashes.

When depression has a biochemical basis, there is always a possibility that it will return. After the birth of our second child, Cherry's depression reoccurred as a postpartum symptom. It was controlled through prescribed medication until her mood was stabilized.

Crafting a new identity.

Recovering people are leaving behind their old disordered identities, and they must find new ones. So much of their time and energy has been invested in the disorder that when they give it up, they may feel anxiety about what will take its place and who they will become. They must redefine—even recreate—who they are. Like the typical adolescent engaged in essentially the same process, the recovering person may experiment, trying on and then discarding several identities looking for one that "fits."

This painful process includes a revision of relationships within the border network. People on the border may find that much of their own identity has been defined by their attempts to cope with the disorder, so now they need a new identity as well. A whole new relational dynamic must be created, especially if—as in our case—the disorder preceded the beginning of the relationship.

Recovering people must find out what it means to be stable instead of moody, open instead of withdrawn, honest instead of deceitful. For their part, border people will discover new roles with that person that are trusting rather than suspicious, collaborative rather than directive, relaxed rather than intense. Parents who were overprotective must learn to relate to their adult children as peers.

Spouses who previously functioned as caretakers must learn to become partners.

An important part of Cherry's search for a new identity was discovering how to express anger appropriately. Her old pattern was to turn her anger inward and punish herself. As she tried to build a new pattern of communicating what she felt, she often found herself irritable, and her expressions of anger were temporarily volatile and extreme.

Eventually that changed as the new, healthy identity emerged. But in the meantime, Dan had to appreciate the process and avoid responding out of anger himself.

Coping with relapses.

Relapses are aftershocks. The big quake is over but tremors jolt our nerves on occasion. Relapses should be seen less as defeats than as stepping stones to health. Sometimes people actually "fall off the wagon" as a way of testing their new identity—checking to see whether the new course they have charted is trustworthy. They are, in a sense, testing their healing. So what do you do when the person you love has a relapse? These insights may help:

1. Don't be shocked.

The recovering person will stumble at times—you can count on it. So be prepared. If you nurture the idealistic notion that there won't ever be a relapse, you'll be like newlyweds who think they'll never have an argument: The first sign of the inevitable conflict will throw you into confusion and despair.

2. Be supportive, not judgmental.

A nurturing, caring attitude will allow the recovering person the sense of freedom and safety necessary for admitting a fall rather than hiding it.

3. Find out what triggered the relapse.

Help the person determine why it happened. Was there some unusual stress? A rejection by a loved one? A failure on the job?

Cultivate a pragmatic attitude. Instead of saying, "Oh, no, we have to start all over again," say, "What can we learn from this experience?"

4. Be patient.

Some studies have shown that over a period of one year, only ten percent of those who try to stop smoking are successful—but over a three-year period, thirty percent are able to quit. This suggests that many people who had "relapses" in their first year eventually went on to overcome their habit, and that's good news. Patience and persistence will be rewarded, so don't give up.

Long-Term Strategies

Even in the good times, when relapses are few and far between, a few long-term strategies can strengthen you as you walk the road to recovery with your loved one. Consider these:

Support groups

Alcoholics Anonymous (AA) is only one of many groups helping recovering people and their families. These groups have proliferated because they offer a safe place to talk about problems and solutions with those who won't judge or condemn—they share the struggler's predicament. Such groups are often established for people in the border network.

Support groups draw on one of the best resources of all: the wisdom of experience. In a report on the use of "multiple family groups" in the treatment of schizophrenia, Drs. William R. McFarlane and Edward Dunne insist that bringing together people from the border network for mutual support has great potential for healing:

> Problems of social isolation, stigmatization, and increased psychological and financial burdens can be addressed by different families offering each other support, expanding the social network, and providing the opportunity to learn from the experiences of others. Studies indicate that the multiple family group

format can reduce the estimated annual relapse rate of forty percent to only eleven percent.

Though the report focuses on studies of schizophrenic patients, the insight is useful for "life on the border" in general. The doctors conclude: "A critical need of families is *access to each other* . . . to learn of other families' successes and failures and to establish a repertoire of coping strategies that are closely tailored to the disorder."[3]

In the back of this book you'll find a partial list of support groups as well as an address for obtaining information about how to start your own if the kind you need is not available in your area. Though most Americans have probably heard of AA, many may not be aware of other groups such as Narcotics Anonymous, Gamblers Anonymous and Sex Addicts Anonymous. We urge you to take advantage of the wisdom and encouragement of people like yourself who have learned from trial and error about the road to recovery.

Journaling

Both of us keep a daily personal journal, and we found it to be a form of therapy in itself during Cherry's recovery. We felt a sense of emotional catharsis when we recorded our thoughts and feelings. In addition, we found that we explored issues in our journals we were not willing to share with anyone else, providing space for speculation, honest reflection, and analysis.

Journaling also served as a mirror for self-examination. Dan discovered, for example, that on a particular day he might deny that he was angry over a particular incident. That night he would write about what happened, and then several days later he would read what he had recorded. If the words of the journal entry had a hostile tone, Dan was able to recognize that he had, in fact, been angry over what happened, and then deal with it.

Keeping a journal record of the recovery process also

helped us understand the patterns that emerged over time so that we could avoid repeating mistakes. Now when we counsel others with a disorder or write about our experiences, we can draw upon our journals for accuracy and detail.

Conflict resolution skills

We noted in chapter 2 that maladaptive behavior is often an attempt to avoid dealing constructively with relationship issues. When this is the case, a disorder's long-term healing must include new and healthier ways of resolving conflict with others.

A thorough discussion of conflict-resolution skills would fill another book. In general, however, the three therapeutic traits we noted earlier—love, honesty, and empathy—go a long way in both resolving and preventing conflicts within the border network. More specifically, cultivation of the positive roles described in chapter 12 and appreciation of personality differences will provide most of the necessary tools for dealing with disagreement.

Sometimes conflict within the network becomes so severe that the parties involved are no longer even listening to each other. In such a highly-charged emotional atmosphere, we recommend choosing what we would call a "witness."

A witness is a third party who cares enough to walk through the conflict with the struggling parties. A good witness is not a counselor who tells you what to do nor a judge who rules on the case. The witness is simply an observer who helps clarify the issues in question so that those locked in conflict are empowered to more easily find their own solution.

Service to others

Life on the border of disorder can turn us inward, constrict our vision of the world and consume all our emotional and physical energies—if we let it. One way to obtain a healthier perspective on our personal struggles and to refocus our attention outward is to invest regular time and perhaps financial resources, even if only a little, in service to others with needs different from our own.

What could be called "volunteer therapy" takes us beyond ourselves and our preoccupation with our own little world of recovery to remind us that we aren't the only ones hurting. If the recovering person joins us in the work, the benefits are multiplied. That person gains a new perspective while deriving a deep satisfaction from helping others. This enhances self-esteem as a sense of personal significance, belonging, and competence are discovered. In addition, volunteer work can assist the recovering person to develop new skills and talents—an important step in creating a new identity.

In 1979 we were involved in founding Mercy Corps International, a humanitarian outreach to people around the world who are hungry, homeless, hurting, and victims of poverty and injustice. As we focused our energies on helping others, our own problems seemed to take on a more manageable scale. We were drawn from total preoccupation with our own struggles to a global vision of needs all around the world. And we knew we could make a difference. It has been a wonderfully refreshing and therapeutic experience to touch the lives of others in crisis.[4]

Lessons We Learned

Looking back on the long, difficult years of Cherry's disorder and subsequent recovery, we have found ourselves asking a question: What have we learned from all this? Has the struggle been redemptive?

The answer is an unqualified yes. We have learned a great deal about ourselves, about each other, and about human nature in general. Dan was forced to recognize that he is human—that there are some things he cannot conquer or even control. Cherry learned that she couldn't be dependent on the praise and approval of others in order to value herself. We learned the meaning of the wedding vows we took as our commitment to each other was

---

[4]For information on Mercy Corps International write to: Mercy Corps International, P.O. Box 9, Portland, OR 97207. Or call 1–800–292–3355.

severely tested "in sickness and in health."

We both learned how complex the human psyche is, how limited our understanding and strength can be, how distorted our perceptions of reality can become. We found that some approaches to life we thought were effective do not really work at all. We discovered not only that we need to love ourselves but also that we need to *know* ourselves—to understand our own feelings, habits, needs, and gifts.

We came to realize how closely entwined our lives are with others—how deep an impact we have on those around us, and they on us. We began to appreciate the value of partnership, interdependence, and compassion. And the power of love.

More than ever, we experienced the grace, mercy, and faithfulness of God.

Choose Hope

Above all, we gained the courage to hope. By this, we don't mean "hope" in the anemic, everyday sense of a half-hearted wish, as in "We hope Cherry gets better." The kind of hope we learned about is better described by Dr. Leo Thomas and Jan Alkire:

> Hope-filled people see their desperate situation but refuse to believe this is all there is to reality. The virtue of hope says that God is dealing with life in ways that surpass our ability to grasp. *Hope, then, is a surrender, a "yes" to faith in God's existence, wisdom, power and, most of all, his love.* God invites us to say yes to an unimaginable future in which the only guarantee is that he will be with us.[5]

Hope, then, is the ultimate form of the healthy "giving up" we discussed before.

You cannot predict with any degree of certainty the outcome of your loved one's struggle. You cannot know how long it will endure or how intense it may be—any more than you can control it. You have no guarantees

---

[5]Leo Thomas, O.P. and Jan Alkire, *Healing as a Parish Ministry* (Notre Dame, Ind.: Ave Maria Press, 1992), p. 138; emphasis is the authors'.

beyond the faith you hold. Nevertheless, you can help transform the border of disorder into a therapeutic environment and the best chance that person has for recovery.

To choose to be part of the healing community is to choose hope.

The choice is yours.

The remarkable and inspiring story of Cherry Boone O'Neill's struggle with and recovery from anorexia nervosa and bulimia has now been updated and re-released:

Starving for Attention
by Cherry Boone O'Neill
LifeCare™ Books, CompCare® Publishers,
Minneapolis, Minnesota
Contact your local bookstore.

Further Resources

Allender, Dan, Ph.D. *The Wounded Heart: Hope for Adult Victims of Childhood Sexual Abuse*. Colorado Springs, Colo.: NavPress, 1990.

Al-Anon Staff. *Al-Anon Faces Alcoholism*. 2nd ed. New York: Al-Anon Family Group Headquarters, Inc.

Bateman, Lana L. *Bible Promises for the Healing Journey*. Westwood, N.J.: Barbour Books, 1991.

Beattie, Melody. *Codependent No More*. San Francisco: Harper/Hazelden, 1987.

———. *Beyond Codependency: And Getting Better All the Time*. San Francisco: Harper/Hazelden, 1989.

Costales, Claire and Barack, Priscilla. *A Secret Hell—Surviving Life With an Alcoholic*. Ventura, Calif.: Regal Books, 1984.

Coyle, Neva. *Overcoming the Dieting Dilemma: What to Do When the Diets Don't Do It*. Minneapolis, Minn.: Bethany House Publishers, 1991.

DeCaussade, Jean-Pierre. *Abandonment to Divine Providence*. New York: Doubleday, 1975.

Ells, Alfred. *One-Way Relationships—When You Love Them More Than They Love You: Healing the Codependency in All of Us*. Nashville, Tenn.: Thomas Nelson Publishers, 1990.

Friends in Recovery. *The Twelve Steps—A Spiritual Journey: A Working Guide for Adult Children From Addictive and Other Dysfunctional Families*. San Diego, Calif.: Tools for Recovery, 1988.

Friends in Recovery. *The Twelve Steps for Christians: From Addictive and Other Dysfunctional Families*. San Diego, Calif.: Tools for Recovery, 1988.

Hemfelt, Dr. Robert; Minirth, Dr. Frank; Meier, Dr. Paul. *Love Is a Choice: Recovery for Codependent Relationships*. Nashville, Tenn.: Thomas Nelson Publishers, 1989.

Keirsey, David; Bates, Marilyn. *Please Understand Me: Character & Temperament Types*. Del Mar, Calif.: Prometheus Nemesis Books, 1978.

LeSourd, Sandra Simpson. *The Compulsive Woman: How to Break the Bonds of Addiction to Food, Television, Sex, Men, Exercise, Shopping, Alcohol, Drugs, Nicotine, and Much More.* Tarrytown, N.Y.: Chosen Books/Revell, 1990.

May, Gerald G., M.D. *Addiction and Grace.* San Francisco: Harper & Row, 1988.

O'Neill, Cherry Boone. *Starving for Attention.* Updated and re-released, Minneapolis, Minn.: CompCare Publishers, LifeCare imprint, 1992.

————. *Dear Cherry: Questions and Answers on Eating Disorders.* New York: Continuum, 1985.

Reiff, Dan W., MPH, RD, and Kathleen Kim Lampson Reiff, Ph.D., *Eating Disorders: Nutrition Therapy in the Recovery Process.* Gaithersburg, Md.: Aspen Publishers, Inc., 1992.

Rinck, Dr. Margaret J. *Can Christians Love Too Much? Breaking the Cycle of Codependency.* Grand Rapids, Mich.: Zondervan, 1989.

Vath, Raymond E., M.D. *Counseling Those With Eating Disorders.* Waco, Tex.: Word Publishing Company, 1986.

Support Groups

To contact the following groups, see the listing in your local telephone directory or newspaper schedule of events, or write them at the addresses below:

Alcoholics Anonymous
World Services, Inc.
468 Park Ave. S.
New York, NY 10016
212/686–1100

Narcotics Anonymous
World Service Office, Inc.
P.O. Box 9999
Van Nuys, CA 91409
818/780–3951

Drugs Anonymous
P.O. Box 473
Ansonia Station
New York, NY 10023
212/874–0700

Cocaine Anonymous
P.O. Box 1367
Culver City, CA 90232
213/559–5833

National Drug Abuse
Information and Referral Line
1–800–662–4357
Cocaine Hotline
1–800-COCAINE

Overeaters Anonymous, Inc.
World Service Office
P.O. Box 92870
Los Angeles, CA 90009
213/657–6252(3)

National Association for Anorexia and Associated Disorders
Box 271
Highland Park, IL 60035
312/831–3438
Eating Disorders Hotline
1–800–382–2832 (US)
212/222–2832 (NY)

Emotions Anonymous (for people with emotional disorders)
International Services
P.O. Box 4245
St. Paul, MN 55104
612/647–9712

Gamblers Anonymous
P.O. Box 17173
Los Angeles, CA 90017
213/386–8789

The Obsessive-Compulsive Disorder Foundation
P.O. Box 9573
Vernon, CT 06535

Relationships Anonymous (for those with a pattern of addictive
and destructive relationships)
P.O. Box 40074
Berkeley, CA 94704

Sexaholics Anonymous
P.O. Box 300
Simi Valley, CA 93062
818/704–9854

Sex and Love Addicts Anonymous
P.O. Box 119
New Town Branch
Boston, MA 02258
617/332–1845

Debtors Anonymous Hotline
212/969–0710

Shopaholics, Limited
212/675–4342
(active in the New York City area)

Smokenders
18551 Von Karman Ave.
Irvine, CA 92715
1–800–828–HELP

Smokers Anonymous
2118 Greenwich St.
San Francisco, CA 94123
415/922–8575

The American Cancer Society
19th W. 56th St.
New York, NY 10019
212/382–2189

Workaholics Anonymous
Westchester Community College
AAB
75 Grasslands Rd.
Valhalla, NY 10595
914/347–3620

Support groups especially for people in the border network:

Gam-Anon/Gamateen
P.O. Box 967
Radio City Station
New York, NY 10019
718/352–1671

Co-Sexaholics Anonymous
P.O. Box 14537
Minneapolis, MN 55414
612/537–0217

Families in Crisis, Inc. (intervention specialists)
7151 Metro Blvd., #225
Edina, MN 55435
612/893–1883

Co-Dependents Anonymous, Inc.
P.O. Box 33577
Phoenix, AZ 85067–3577
602/277–7991

Al-Anon Family Group Hdq., Inc.
P.O. Box 182
Midtown Station
New York, NY 10018
212/302–7240

Families Anonymous, Inc.
P.O. Box 528
Van Nuys, CA 91408
818/989–7841

National Domestic Violence Hotline
1–800–333–7233

National Association for Children of Alcoholics
31706 Coast Highway, Suite 201
South Laguna, CA 90504

Children of Alcoholics Foundation
P.O. Box 4185
Grand Central Station
New York, NY 10163

The National Clearinghouse for Alcohol and Drug Information
P.O. Box 2345
Rockville, MD 20852
301/468–2600

National Federation of Parents for Drug-Free Youth
1423 N. Jefferson
Springfield, MO 65802
414/836–3709

National Suicide Assistance 24-Hour Hotline
1–800–333–4444

Christian Support Groups:

Alcoholics Victorious
National Headquarters
P.O. Box 10364
Tigard, OR 97210
503/245–9629

Liontamers
2801 North Brea Blvd.
Fullerton, CA 92635–2799
714/529–5544

Substance Abusers Victorious
One Cascade Plaza
Akron, OH 44308

A Twelve-Step Support Group outline for starting your own group is contained in *The Twelve Steps—A Spiritual Journey* available from:

Tools for Recovery
1201 Knoxville St.
San Diego, CA 92110
1–800–873–8384

For information about the location of alcohol and drug treatment centers, write:

International Publishing Group
Alcoholism and Addiction Magazine
4959 Commerce Parkway
Cleveland, OH 44128
216/464–1210

Christian treatment programs:

Minirth-Meier Clinic
2100 N. Collins Blvd.
Richardson, TX 75080
1–800–229–3000

New Life Treatment Centers
570 Glenneyre Ave. Suite 107
Laguna Beach, CA 92651
1–800–227–LIFE

Rapha
Box 580355
Houston, TX 77258
1–800–227–2657
In Texas: 1–800–445–2657

For referrals to Christian medical professionals in your area, contact:

Christian Medical and Dental Society
P.O. Box 830689
Richardson, TX 75083–0689
214/783–8384